CASAS TEST PREP STUDENT BOOK

FOR

READING GOALS FORM 905R/906R

LEVEL C

Preparing Adult Learners for CASAS
Reading GOALS Tests and for Workforce
and College Reading

By Coaching for Better Learning, LLC

CASAS TEST PREP
STUDENT BOOK FOR READING GOALS
FORMS 905R/906R LEVEL C

Preparing Adult Learners
for CASAS Reading GOALS Tests
&
Workforce and College Reading

COACHING FOR BETTER LEARNING LLC

COACHING FOR BETTER LEARNING

TABLE OF CONTENTS

INTRODUCTION

This test prep student book is designed to develop adult learners' academic reading skills, preparing them for CASAS Reading GOALS Level C Forms 905R/906R tests and vocational training admission reading tests. In other words, it presents academic reading activities that help adult education and workforce programs, along with their learners, meet the Workforce Innovation and Opportunity Act (WIOA) reading expectations.

The reading exercises and answer keys in this student book cover CASAS Reading GOALS Level C standards and College and Career Readiness (CCR) reading standards and content. For example, each lesson focuses on three main areas: ***vocabulary, reading comprehension skills and higher-order reading skills.***

The reading passages presented are from various sources—journal articles, newspaper clippings and nonfiction and fiction books—covering a wide range of topics. Learners will also be guided to reflect on what they have learned after completing the practice tests at the end of the lessons.

Reading Strategies

This student reading textbook covers and teaches the following reading strategies:

- *Using Background Knowledge*
- *Making Inferences and Predictions*
- *Constructing Visual Imagery*
- *Identifying Text Structures and Cohesive Devices*
- *Understanding Unfamiliar Vocabulary*
- *Reading Long Passages*
- *Learning Nonfiction Text Features*
- *Understanding Figurative Language*
- *Reading for Main Ideas*
- *Understanding Main Ideas and Finding Evidence*
- *Understanding What You Read*
- *Analyzing the Narrator and Point of View (POV)*

The book is designed for adult learners as an instructional guide for developing reading comprehension skills. It offers academic reading strategies to help learners become more active, strategic and purposeful readers. These strategies will also help learners understand and remember what they read.

Reading is an active thinking process. Therefore, this manual encourages learners to engage actively with texts by predicting, making connections and inferences, asking and answering questions, and completing the comprehension activities.

Additionally, the text provides practice exercises for using the reading strategies to access different types of texts, e.g., science, social studies, technical and literary. The lessons emphasize text complexity, evidence and knowledge.

All the reading strategies are presented with examples, pictures and text. These learning aids will help you understand each strategy and how it works and give you hands-on practice. As you read, study and work through these examples, you will build the confidence to succeed. **You will become a strategic reader**. Let's get started!

Before we start, let's start you off by filling in the box below:

WHAT DO I KNOW ABOUT READING COMPREHENSION?	WHAT DO I WANT TO KNOW?

LESSON 1
TECHNIQUES FOR IMPROVING YOUR READING COMPREHENSION

Before you can improve, you need to understand how you read to determine the best strategy. Do you lose concentration easily? Is the passage you are reading difficult to comprehend? Is your vocabulary holding you back? Let's look at a couple of techniques you can use to boost your reading comprehension.

1. Assess how you are reading.

Begin by choosing passages from unfamiliar writings and set a timer. As you read, try to notice when you start losing focus. If you notice you lose concentration after 15 minutes, acknowledge this, then push yourself next time. Push yourself by increasing the time and building your reading stamina.

2. Assess your vocabulary.

As you read, make a list of unfamiliar words. Search for the meanings in a dictionary and design some helpful flashcards. Additionally, you can use numerous resources and mobile apps to help improve your vocabulary, such as "Word of the Day" apps. Finally, use these new words in your written and verbal communication. Doing this helps keep them in your long-term memory, ready for use next time.

3. Stop and think.

If you lose focus or get confused, stop and think about what you've read. Without re-reading, jot down some key points. After, skim through the text to compare the details with what you have written. Keep this information in mind as you continue to read. The more you can understand the text in your own words, the better you'll be able to connect the various sections of the writing.

4. Use what you already know to determine what you are reading.

If you struggle to understand some words, you can use the provided contextual clues and interpret the words in that way. Think about the title of the composition or the included graphics and images. Do they hint at what the text is about? Also, make a connection between your life experiences and the subject of the text. Doing this will allow you to make connections you may assume are not present.

5. Practice, practice, practice!

Reading is fun. Or it can be. Dedicate some time to both guided and relaxed reading sessions. Why? Because if reading starts to feel like a chore or something you have to do, you may lack the motivation to improve your weaknesses.

6. **Try non-linear reading.**

If a passage is particularly tricky to understand, make a note. Then, you can either skim through the next couple sentences or revert to the sentences before the problematic text. Sometimes, we understand texts better if we don't read linearly. Skimming forward or backward may help to access basic information about a text.

Finally, here are some more useful techniques:

- Reading problematic passages aloud helps you internalize what you are reading and get rid of the "mental block" that may be slowing you down.
- Sometimes, reading the questions first may help to decipher quickly what you should look out for in the text. In this way, as you read the text, the questions are at the back of your mind, and you can mark down the possible answers as you move along.
- At the beginning stages, keep a reading journal to track and reflect on your progress.

ACTIVITY

1. What do you think your reading strengths and weaknesses are?

   _____

   _____

   _____

   _____

2. Which two techniques listed in this chapter will be useful to you? Why?

   _____

   _____

   _____

   _____

LESSON 2
UNDERSTANDING UNFAMILIAR VOCABULARY

By the end of this lesson, you will discover and uncover a range of unfamiliar keywords and their role in sentence construction and meaning. We will focus on how you can use surrounding words, root words and "breaking-a-word down" as helpful strategies.

Surrounding Words

If you come across an unfamiliar word within a sentence, look at the words used before and after the unfamiliar word. Ask yourself how it is used. Is it a verb, an adjective or something else? Thinking about similar words that may be more familiar can also help.

'I remembered the case well, for it was one in which Holmes had taken an interest on account of the peculiar <u>ferocity</u> of the crime and the wanton brutality which had marked all the actions of the assassin. The commutation of his death sentence had been due to some doubts as to his complete sanity, so <u>atrocious</u> was his conduct. Our wagonette had topped a rise and in front of us rose the huge expanse of the moor, mottled with gnarled and craggy cairns and tors. A cold wind swept down from it and set us shivering. Somewhere there, on that <u>desolate</u> plain, was lurking this fiendish man, hiding in a burrow like a wild beast, his heart full of <u>malignancy</u> against the whole race which had cast him out. It needed but this to complete the grim suggestiveness of the barren waste, the chilling wind, and the darkling sky. Even Baskerville fell silent and pulled his overcoat more closely around him.'

An excerpt from The Hound of the Baskervilles
by Sir Arthur Conan Doyle (1902)

In the above excerpt, the underlined words may be unfamiliar. Let's take the example of the word "<u>malignancy</u>." Other words in the sentence suggest that "<u>malignancy</u>" portrays a negative feeling because the man was angry at people who had been mean to him.

EXERCISE 1

Using a dictionary, what do the other three words mean? Compare with a classmate.

1. *Ferocity* means _____

2. *Atrocious* means _____

3. *Desolate* means _____

Looking for the Root Word

Think of the root word as the foundation of a word from which other words "grow." The root word can be found anywhere within the word.

1. My mother and I have a **symbiotic** relationship.

The writer uses the word **symbiotic.** The root of the word is -**bio**-, which means life. Based on the way the word is used in the sentence, you understand that the writer and their mother have a mutually beneficial living arrangement.

2. I'll be writing my **autobiography** in a few days.

The writer uses the word **autobiography.** The root word is **auto-** which means self. Based on the way the word is used in the sentence, you understand that the writer will be writing a book based on their life. There is another root word. Can you identify it?

- What is the other root word in this sentence and what does it mean?

_____

3. Charlie's **sadness** affected us all.

The writer uses the word **sadness.** The root of the word is "sad" which is a state of being unhappy. Based on the way the word is used in the sentence, you understand that the other people were affected by Charlie's emotions.

Breaking a Word Down

The study of the origins of English vocabulary and how meanings have changed over time is known as **Etymology**. Understanding the history of unfamiliar words can help in breaking down their meanings. A prefix is added before the root of the word and a suffix is added at the end of the root word. Both the prefix and suffix change the word's meaning.

Prefix: This is a word part added at the beginning of a word. Below are examples.

1. It is **impossible** to run 42 miles without training.

The writer uses the word **impossible**. The prefix **"im-"** is originally Latin for **"not"**; therefore, "impossible" means **"not possible."** From the way the word is used in the sentence, you understand that the writer is saying it is not possible to run that distance without getting some physical training.

2. "We are having **triplets**!" Jack couldn't believe his luck.

The writer uses the word **triplets**. The prefix **"tri-"** is originally Latin for "three"; therefore, "triplets" means "three children." From the way the word is used in the sentence, you understand that Jack and his partner are having three children.

Suffix: This is a word part added at the end of a word. Below are examples.

1. John has such a nasty **attitude**. I can't stand him.

The writer uses the word **attitude**. The suffix **"-tude"** means "as a result of an action." From the way the word is used in the sentence, you understand that the writer does not like John because of his mannerisms.

2. Julia received an **internship** position at Biddles & Biddles law firm. Her **supervisor** will be Mr. Biddle himself, one of the partners.

The writer used the words **internship** and **supervisor**. The suffix **"-ship"** means "position held," and **"-or"** means "one who performs the action." From the way the words are used in the sentence, you understand that Julia will be working at the law firm and managed by Mr. Biddle.

PRACTICE EXERCISE

"Between me and the other world, there is an unasked question: <u>unasked</u> by some through <u>feelings</u> of <u>delicacy</u>; by others through the <u>difficulty</u> of <u>rightly framing</u> it. All, nevertheless, flutter round it. They approach me in a <u>half-hesitant</u> sort of way, eye me curiously or <u>compassionately</u>, and then, instead of saying <u>directly</u>, how does it feel to be a problem they say, I know an excellent colored man in my town; or, I fought at Mechanicsville; or, Do not these Southern <u>outrages</u> make your blood boil? At these I smile, or am interested, or reduce the boiling to a simmer, as the occasion may require. To the real question, How does it feel to be a problem? I answer seldom a word."

————

An excerpt from The Souls of Black Folk *by W. E. B. Du Bois (1903)*

1. What do you understand from the passage above? Discuss with a classmate.

_____

_____

2. From the text above, what is the meaning of the word **unasked**?

_____

_____

3. What clues did you use to come up with that definition?

_____

_____

4. Label the following items according to their types:

Un-	-ask-	-ed

5. Referring to the underlined words in the excerpt, fill in the table below:

WHICH WORDS HAVE PREFIXES?	WHICH WORDS HAVE SUFFIXES?

6. What can be inferred from the use of the word **disliked** in the passage below?

Mr. Brainley disliked taking walks around his neighborhood. He hated running into the group of teenage boys that hung about the streets with nothing better to do than hustle people. Occasionally, though, he would visit his local Turkish kebab takeaway to chat with his friend, Mr. Emin.

_____

_____

7. The words *occasionally* and *teenage* contain suffixes. Identify what they are.

_____

_____

8. Write down the possible meanings of the suffixes below. Use your experience and knowledge to guess what they may be. Discuss your answers with a classmate.

a. Neighbor-*hood*:

_____

b. Turk-*ish*:

_____

9. What do these italicized words mean?

a. Pablo always showed *animosity* toward his teachers by throwing spitballs and mouthing off, but his sister, Mary, was kind and sweet.

_____

_____

b. The sorcerer's *minions* were willing to complete any task they were given as long as evil was not conjured upon them.

_____

_____

c. We always listen to my great-aunt because she is *venerable*, but we ignore my niece's advice because she's only six.

_____

_____

d. "Busy as a bee" and "quiet as a mouse" are *hackneyed* phrases—they're used all the time.

_____

_____

10. Break down each of the following words and suggest what is the root word and prefix/suffix.

WORD	PREFIX	ROOT WORD	SUFFIX	MEANING
Megaphone				
Incapable				
Psychology				
Hypercritical				
Productive				
Excellence				
Contradictory				

REFLECTION ON LEARNING

Answer the following reflection questions, and feel free to discuss your responses with your teacher or classmate.

- What reading idea or strategy did you learn from this section?

- What new concepts did you learn?

- What methods did you work on in this section?

- What aspect of this section is still not 100 percent clear for you?

- What do you want your teacher to know?

LESSON 3

IDENTIFYING TEXT STRUCTURES AND COHESIVE DEVICES

When you are reading, you will notice that sentences are constructed in different ways. Sentence structures allow writers to shape their writings in ways that convey clear meaning. By the end of this chapter, we will cover four types of structures: <u>cause and effect</u>, <u>compare and contrast</u>, <u>sequence and chronological order,</u> and <u>problem and solution</u>. We will also examine the importance of using cohesive words when creating these different text structures.

Cause and Effect

This type of text structure involves mentioning what happened (the cause) and why it happened (the effect).

Example:

*Elia switched off the lights. (**the cause**)*
*The room became dark. (**the effect**)*

From the example above, you understand that the room became dark due to Elia's action.

*Andy broke his foot. (**the cause**)*
*The nurse put it in a cast. (**the effect**)*

From the example above, you understand that Andy needed a cast because he broke his leg.

EXERCISE 1

What do you understand from the sentences below?

1. *Many Javan Rhinos have been killed. (**the cause**)*
    *Javan Rhinos are extinct. (**the effect**)*

_____

2. *The employees were on strike. (**the cause**)*
    *The business needed to close for a month. (**the effect**)*

_____

Such short sentences are not usually included within a text, and writers usually use ***cohesive devices*** to link sentences together. Cohesive devices can be described as **linking phrases or words**.

Examples:

*Elia switched off the lights, and **consequently,** the room became dark.*
*Andy broke his foot, **so** the nurse put it in a cast.*

Sometimes the word order can be reversed so that the effect comes before the cause, with a cohesive device linking them together.

*The room became dark **because** Elia switched off the lights.*
*The nurse put Andy's foot in a cast **since** he broke it.*

EXERCISE 2

1. Name the cohesive device used to link these sentences:

    The boys played in the rain. Therefore, they got sick.

    _____

2. Is the following sentence an appropriate rewrite of the sentence above? Why?

    The boys got sick because they played in the rain.

    _____

Compare and Contrast

This type of sentence structure shows the similarities (comparison) and differences (contrast) between two or more people, things, places or ideas. Here are a couple of examples:

a. *Yana was born in Egypt. Kelly was born in Egypt.*

Through these statements, you understand that Yana and Kelly share the same birthplace, which is Egypt. Here, the statements can be rewritten in the following ways:

    Both *Yana and Kelly were born in Egypt.*
    Yana, **as well as** *Kelly, was born in Egypt.*

b. *Frank can run 10 miles. James can run 20 miles.*

    These sentences can be rewritten in the following ways:

    While *Frank can run 10 miles, James can run 20 miles.*
    Frank can run 10 miles; **however,** *James can run 20 miles.*

While reading, look for sentences with this kind of structure as they are very common.

EXERCISE 3

1. Use "as opposed to" to link the sentences below:

    - I took a step back and evaluated the situation.
    - I didn't want to make an assumption and make things worse.

    _____

2. Use "just like" to link the sentences below:

    - Katherine has worn green Adidas shoes.
    - Felix has worn green Adidas shoes.

    _____

Sequence and Chronological Order

A writer uses this type of sentence construction to organize events or inform readers about a series of events. In fiction, a story is a journey through time, and the events in it are usually arranged in order. Every story has a beginning, a middle and an end.

Pablo Picasso is known for his abstract art style. His father was also an artist and started training him when he was seven. When Picasso was 13, he was so good that his father quit painting to support his son's vision. At 16, Picasso moved to Madrid to attend the Royal Academy of San Fernando.

From the above writing, you can infer that

   a. At age 7, Picasso's father began to train him.
   b. When Picasso was 13, his father quit painting.
   c. At the age of 16, Picasso went to art school.

Read the following excerpt from *Personal Memoirs Of U.S. Grant* by Ulysses S. Grant (1885)

At last, the preparations were complete and orders were issued for the advance to begin on the **8th of March**. General Taylor had an army of not more than three thousand men. One battery, the siege guns and all the convalescent troops were sent on by water to Brazos Santiago, **at the mouth of the Rio Grande.** A guard was left back at Corpus Christi to look after public property and take care of those who were too sick to be removed. The remainder of the army, probably not more than twenty-five hundred men, was divided into three brigades, with the cavalry independent. Colonel Twiggs, with seven companies of dragoons and a battery of light artillery, **moved on the 8th.** He was followed by the three infantry brigades, **with a day's interval** between the commands. Thus, the rear brigade did not move from Corpus Christi **until the 11th of March.** In view of the immense bodies of men moved on the same day over narrow roads, through dense forests and across large streams, in our late war, it seems strange now that a body of fewer than three thousand men should have been broken into four columns, separated **by a day's march.**

From the above excerpt, you can infer the following things:

   a. Orders to advance were delivered on the 8th of March.
   b. General Taylor's army had less than three thousand men.
   c. They were sent to Brazos Santiago.
   d. One guard was left at Corpus Christi to take care of public property and care for the sick.
   e. Less than two hundred men were divided into three brigades.
   f. Colonel Twiggs' army moved on the 8th as well.
   g. Three infantry brigades followed Colonel Twiggs' army on the 9th.
   h. The rear brigade moved on the 11th.
   i. Both General Taylor's and Colonel Twiggs' armies were less than three thousand men.

EXERCISE 4

Read the passage below from the "Revolutionary War Turning Points: Saratoga and Valley Forge" article by Adena Barnette.

> Intent on the first, British General, John Burgoyne, led a force of eight thousand troops southward through the Hudson Valley towards the town of Saratoga, New York during the summer and fall of 1777. On September 19 and again on October 7, American forces led by General Horatio Gates clashed with the British Army. By October 8, the British forces totaled less than five thousand. The American Continentals pursued, and on October 17, twenty thousand surrounded the British, leaving Burgoyne with no choice other than to formally surrender. This decisive victory at Saratoga helped persuade the French to enter the war in February 1778, providing the money, supplies, and troops needed to turn the tide to American victory.

1. What happened in the summer and fall of 1777?

2. What happened in February 1778?

3. Draw a timeline and list the events of the passage in chronological order in your notebook.

4. What can you infer from the passage?

Problem and Solution

Writers use this text structure to create an organizational pattern where information is expressed as a dilemma or concerning issue (a problem), and something was, can be, or should be done to remedy this issue (solution or attempted solution).

Example:

> *Karly sprained her ankle during football practice. She was rushed to the emergency room. The doctor put ice on her to reduce the swelling and the pain. The doctor also told Karly that putting ice helps to reduce internal bleeding.*

From the writing above, you can infer that swelling and pain associated with a sprained ankle can be reduced by placing an ice pack on it.

> *Having a cold can make you lethargic. Additionally, coughing makes it hard to fall asleep, and a sore throat is painful. It is no fun at all! Therefore, one should try some tea with honey in it. The honey will soothe the throat and treat the symptoms.*

From the excerpt above, you can infer that cold symptoms can be minimized using home-remedy treatments such as honey.

EXERCISE 5

Read the following excerpt from *Common Sense* by Thomas Paine (1776):

> I have never met with a man, either in England or America, who hath not confessed his opinion, that a separation between the countries, would take place one time or other: And there is no instance, in which we have shewn less judgment, than in endeavoring to describe, what we call, the ripeness or fitness of the Continent for independence.
>
> As all men allow the measure, and vary only in their opinion of the time, let us, in order to remove mistakes, take a general survey of things, and endeavor, if possible, to find out the *very* time. But we need not go far, the inquiry ceases at once, for, the *time hath found us*. The general concurrence, the glorious union of all things prove the fact.

This portion of the text relates to the separation of England and America, which happened two years after the book's release. From the above excerpt, you can infer that the writer is suggesting analyzing facts before mistakes are made.

What else can you infer from the passage? Discuss with a classmate.

_____

PRACTICE EXERCISE

1. Read the short passage below.

    Kate's performance was affected by her increasing health issues. Consequently, her supervisor sat down with her to discuss ways the company could accommodate her. As a result, she has a flexible work schedule and sometimes works from home.

    a. Identify the cause and effect linking words.

    _____

    b. Which statements show the cause and which show the effects?

    _____

    _____

2. Read the following excerpt from *The Hound of the Baskervilles* by Sir Arthur Conan Doyle (1902) and answer the following questions:

    "No, sir, no; though I am happy to have had the opportunity of doing that <u>as well</u>. I came to you, Mr. Holmes, <u>because</u> I recognized that I am myself an unpractical man and <u>because</u> I am suddenly confronted with a most serious and extraordinary problem. Recognizing, as I do, that you are the second highest expert in Europe—"
    "Indeed, sir! May I inquire who has the honor to be the first?" asked Holmes <u>with</u> some asperity.
    "To the man of precisely scientific mind the work of Monsieur Bertillon must always appeal strongly."
    "Then had you not better consult him?"
    "I said, sir, to the precisely scientific mind. But as a practical man of affairs it is <u>acknowledged</u> that you stand alone. I trust, sir, that I have not inadvertently—"

a. What can you infer from the passage above?

_____

_____

b. Name two ways the writer has used the "compare-and-contrast" structure. Support your answer.

_____

_____

3. Analyze the structure of the partial sentence below. Which has been addressed first, the cause or effect? Support your answer.

   '....it was not merely for the purpose of examining my skull that you have done me the honor to call here last night and again today?'
   (Excerpt from *The Hound of the Baskervilles* by Sir Arthur Conan Doyle, 2008)

_____

_____

4. Read the passage below.

   All matter, all things can be changed in two ways: chemically and physically. Both chemical and physical changes affect the state of matter. Physical changes are those that do not change the make-up or identity of the matter. For example, clay will bend or flatten if squeezed, but it will still be clay. Changing the shape of clay is a physical change, and does not change the matter's identity. Chemical changes turn the matter into a new kind of matter with different properties.

a. What type of text structure is it? _____

b. How do you know this? Explain your answer.

_____

_____

5. **Read the following excerpt from *The Voyager of the Beagle* by Charles Dickens (1839)**

ST. PAUL'S ROCKS.—In crossing the Atlantic, we hove-to during the morning of February 16th, close to the island of St. Paul's. This cluster of rocks is situated in 0 degree. 58' north latitude, and 29 degrees. 15' west longitude. It is 540 miles distant from the coast of America, and 350 from the island of Fernando Noronha. The highest point is only fifty feet above the level of the sea, and the entire circumference is under three-quarters of a mile. This small point rises abruptly out of the depths of the ocean. Its mineralogical constitution is not simple; in some parts, the rock is of a cherty, in others of a felspathic nature, including thin veins of serpentine. It is a remarkable fact that all the many small islands, lying far from any continent, in the Pacific, Indian, and Atlantic Oceans, with the exception of the Seychelles and this little point of rock, are, I believe, composed either of coral or of erupted matter. The volcanic nature of these oceanic islands is evidently an extension of that law, and the effect of those same causes, whether chemical or mechanical, from which it results that a vast majority of the volcanoes now in action stand either near sea-coasts or as islands in the midst of the sea.

a. When did the writer arrive on the island of St. Paul's? _____

b. What is the circumference of the island of St. Paul's? _____

c. What does the writer say has caused islands like St Paul's to be composed of either coral or erupted matter? _____

d. Where are the vast majority of volcanoes situated? _____

6. **Read the passage below.**

Many people are confused about why our economy went to shambles in 2008. The crisis was actually the result of a combination of many complex factors. First, easy credit conditions allowed people who were high-risk or unworthy of credit to borrow, and even people who had no income were eligible for large loans. Second, banks would bundle these toxic loans and sell them as packages on the financial market. Third, large insurance firms backed these packages, misrepresenting these high-risk loans as safe investments. All of these factors created bubbles of speculation.

a. What type of text structure is it? _____

b. How do you know this? Explain your answer.

_____

_____

REFLECTION ON LEARNING

Answer the following reflection questions, and feel free to discuss your responses with your teacher or classmate.

- What reading idea or strategy did you learn from this section?

- What new concepts did you learn?

- What methods did you work on in this section?

- What aspect of this section is still not 100 percent clear for you?

- What do you want your teacher to know?

LESSON 4

APPLYING BACKGROUND KNOWLEDGE

Do you remember your favorite childhood game? Do you remember the last book you read and why you liked/hated it? All these experiences and events form our background knowledge. By the end of this lesson, you will be able to use prior knowledge to make reading easier. We will look at text-to-self, text-to-text, and text-to-world connections.

Text-to-Self

We use words every day to convey meaning in informal and formal situations. When you make a personal connection to a text, you make a text-to-self connection. Text-to-self connections make the reading relatable and more important for the reader.

When reading a text, make a personal connection using phrases such as the following:	*This reminds me of ....* *That's how my sister....* *My college football coach used to....* *I remember....* *I tried to do something like that when....* *I act like that when....*

Read this excerpt from *Pride and Prejudice* by Jane Austen (1813).

Now and then they were honored with a call from her ladyship, and nothing escaped her observation that was passing in the room during these visits. She examined into their employments, looked at their work, and advised them to do it differently; found fault with the arrangement of the furniture; or detected the housemaid in negligence; and if she accepted any refreshment, seemed to do it only for the sake of finding out that Mrs. Collins's joints of meat were too large for her family.

I would make a **text-to-self connection** about Mrs. Collins (her ladyship) in the following way: ***This reminds me of*** *my mother's strictness when I was growing up. Before bedtime on every school night, she would ensure our homework was completed to her satisfaction, and our uniform was laid out, ready for the following day.*

EXERCISE 1

Can you make a connection with the above excerpt?

_____

_____

Text-to-Text

Text-to-text connections involve linking two or more different texts you have read. When making a text-to-text connection, you find what is similar and familiar in these texts. Finding the similarities makes learning and understanding easier.

Read the following excerpts carefully:

Mr. Utterson, the lawyer, was a man of a rugged countenance that was never lighted by a smile; cold, scanty and embarrassed in discourse; backward in sentiment; lean, long, dusty, dreary and yet somehow lovable. ____ An excerpt from *The Strange Case of Dr. Jekyll and Mr. Hyde* by Robert Louis Stevenson (1866)	The appearance of our visitor was a surprise to me, since I had expected a typical country practitioner. He was a very tall, thin man, with a long nose like a beak, which jutted out between two keen, grey eyes, set closely together and sparkling brightly from behind a pair of gold-rimmed glasses. ____ An excerpt from *The Hound of the Baskervilles by* Sir Arthur Conan Doyle (1902)

How do these two texts connect? To give you some ideas, here are some examples of the connections:

1. Both texts are observations.
2. Both texts describe a man's appearance.

EXERCISE 2

Can you make any other text-to-text connections from the above excerpts?

_____

_____

Text-to-World:

Text-to-world connections are often the most difficult to make. When making such a connection, think about what is going on in the world today. How is the text you are reading similar to events that are happening in the world?

Read the excerpt below from *The Strange Case of Dr. Jekyll and Mr. Hyde* by Robert Louis Stevenson (1886).

It was a wild, cold, seasonable night of March, with a pale moon, lying on her back as though the wind had tilted her, and flying wrack of the most diaphanous and lawny texture. The wind made talking difficult, and flecked the blood into the face. It seemed to have swept the streets unusually bare of passengers, besides; for Mr. Utterson thought he had never seen that part of London so deserted. He could have wished it otherwise; never in his life had he been conscious of so sharp a wish to see and touch his fellow-creatures; for struggle as he might, there was borne in upon his mind a crushing anticipation of calamity.

How can you make a text-to-world connection? Think about what has been happening in the world.

To give you some ideas, here are some examples of the connections:

a. In the recent past, COVID-19 led to the government mandating us to go into lockdown for several weeks.
b. Many were in isolation by themselves.
c. We could only go outside if we had to shop, exercise or work.

EXERCISE 3

Can you make any other text-to-world connections with the above excerpt?

_____

_____

Final Thoughts

When reading, ask yourself the following questions:

- Does anything here remind me of something that happened in my life?
- What do I know now about this topic that I didn't know before reading this article?
- How can I use my background knowledge to predict what might happen next?
- What does this article tell me about the world?
- Do I agree with what the author says, or do I disagree? Why?

PRACTICE EXERCISES

Read the excerpt below and answer the questions that follow.

> After a while, finding that nothing more happened, she decided on going into the garden at once; but, alas for poor Alice! when she got to the door, she found she had forgotten the little golden key, and when she went back to the table for it, she found she could not possibly reach it: she could see it quite plainly through the glass, and she tried her best to climb up one of the legs of the table, but it was too slippery; and when she had tired herself out with trying, the poor little thing sat down and cried.
>
> An excerpt from *Alice's Adventures in Wonderland* by Lewis Carroll (1865)

1. Using the phrases below, make two text-to-self connections.

a. *I act like the character when I* _____

_____

b. *This reminds me of when* _____

_____

c. Make one text-to-text connection.

_____

_____

2. Read the excerpts below and answer the following questions:

"How despicably I have acted!" she cried; "I, who have prided myself on my discernment! I, who have valued myself on my abilities! Who have often disdained the generous candor of my sister, and gratified my vanity in useless or blameable mistrust! How humiliating is this discovery! Yet, how just a humiliation! Had I been in love, I could not have been more wretchedly blind! But vanity, not love, has been my folly. Pleased with the preference of one, and offended by the neglect of the other, on the very beginning of our acquaintance, I have courted prepossession and ignorance, and driven reason away, where either were concerned. Till this moment I never knew myself."	There have been decorators and furnishers up from Plymouth, and it is evident that our friend has large ideas and means to spare no pains or expense to restore the grandeur of his family. When the house is renovated and refurnished, all that he will need will be a wife to make it complete. Between ourselves there are pretty clear signs that this will not be wanting if the lady is willing, for I have seldom seen a man more infatuated with a woman than he is with our beautiful neighbor, Miss Stapleton. And yet the course of true love does not run quite as smoothly as one would under the circumstances expect. Today, for example, its surface was broken by a very unexpected ripple, which has caused our friend considerable perplexity and annoyance.
An excerpt from *Pride and Prejudice* by Jane Austen (1813)	An excerpt from *The Hound of the Baskervilles* by Sir Arthur Conan Doyle (1902)

a. What comes to mind when you read these two excerpts?

_____

_____

_____

b. Can you make a text-to-text connection?

_____

_____

_____

c. Can you make at least two text-to-world connections?

_____

_____

_____

3. Look at the picture below and answer the questions that follow.

a. What text-to-self connection can you make with the above picture?

_____

_____

b. What text-to-world connection can you make from the above picture?

_____

_____

REFLECTION ON LEARNING

Answer the following reflection questions, and feel free to discuss your responses with your teacher or classmate.

- What reading idea or strategy did you learn from this section?

- What new concepts did you learn?

- What methods did you work on in this section?

- What aspect of this section is still not 100 percent clear for you?

- What do you want your teacher to know?

LESSON 5
INTERPRETING FIGURATIVE LANGUAGE

Figurative language is used to help the reader visualize what the writer is describing, making the writing come alive. In this lesson, you will learn about five forms of figurative language: <u>symbolism</u>, <u>alliteration</u>, <u>hyperbole</u>, <u>simile</u> and <u>metaphor</u>.

Symbolism

With symbolism, something takes on a meaning beyond what it actually is. Think of a symbol as something tangible, something you can hold or touch with your hand. If it is something you cannot touch, eliminate it as a possible symbol:

> *Lona worked like an* **ox** *to complete her assignment on time.*
> *She ended up getting a good grade as a result.*

From the above example, you understand that because of Lona's actions, she received a good mark on her assignment. You can deduce this is because she **worked hard** on it. Thus the word **'ox'** symbolizes **hard work**.

> *'All the world's a <u>stage</u>, And all the men and women merely <u>players</u>; they have their <u>exits and their entrances</u>; and one man in his time plays many parts.'*

> — An excerpt from Shakespeare's play, *As You Like It (1599)*

From the above example, you understand that the poem talks about the **different roles people perform in their lives**. "A stage" here symbolizes the world, and "players" is a symbol for human beings.

> *"My love for Linton is like the* **<u>foliage in the woods</u>**. *Time will change it; I'm well aware, as winter changes the trees. My love for Heathcliff resembles the* **eternal rocks** *beneath a source of little visible delight, but necessary."*
>
> _____
> An excerpt from *Wuthering Heights* by Emily Bronte (1847)

From the above example, you understand that the speaker is <u>**describing her love for Linton and Heathcliff in two different ways**</u>. You can infer from the other surrounding words that the speaker prefers Linton to Heathcliff. Therefore, you can guess that <u>**"foliage in the woods"**</u> refers to a civilized relationship while <u>**"external rocks"**</u> refers to a problematic relationship.

EXERCISE 1

What do the following phrases/words usually symbolize?

1. The bullied boy's <u>stuffed toy</u> lay ripped and tattered on the floor.

   _____

2. Lisa blushed when she received the <u>red flowers</u> from Chris.

Alliteration

This is a literary device in which a series of words begin with the same consonant sound. The best way to spot alliteration is to sound out the sentence, looking for the words with identical beginning consonant sounds. These words can be used to enhance rhythm and create a beat in poetry.

Popular examples include:
   a. **Busy** as a **bee**
   b. **Dead** as a **doornail**
   c. Make a **mountain** out of a **molehill**
   d. **She sells seashells** by the **sea-shore**
   e. **Peter Piper picked a peck of pickled peppers**.

*"When **g**riping **g**rief the heart doth wound, and **d**oleful **d**umps the mind oppress…"*
(Spoken by Peter in Act 4, Scene 5)

-An excerpt from *Romeo and Juliet* by Shakespeare (1597)

From the example above, alliteration is found in the **"g"** and **"d"** sounds to emphasize the intensity of depression.

*There are some nights when, sleep plays **coy**,*
aloof and disdainful.
*And all the wiles, that I **employ** to win*
*its service to my **side**, are useless as wounded **pride**,*
and much more painful.

A poem excerpt from *Insomniac* by Maya Angelou (No date)

From the above example, the repetition of the words -*oy* in the words "c**oy**" and "empl**oy**", and -*ide* in "s**ide**" and "pr**ide**" give this poem a rhythm.

EXERCISE 2

Can you think of other famous alliteration examples?

_____

_____

Hyperbole

These are statements that exaggerate to emphasize a point. They are attention-grabbers and can help a writer achieve a dramatic effect. However, they can quickly become clichés and lose their dramatic effect if overused. Here are some good examples:

   a. I'm so hungry that I could **eat a horse**.
   b. She's as **old as the hills**.
   c. I walked **a million miles** to get here.

    d. She can hear **a pin drop a mile away**.

*"A day was twenty-four hours long but seemed longer. There was **no** hurry, for there was **nowhere** to go, **nothing** to buy and **no money** to buy it with, **nothing** to see outside the boundaries of Maycomb County."*

_____
An excerpt from *To Kill a Mockingbird* by Harper Lee (1960)

From the above excerpt, you can understand that the writer uses hyperbole to emphasize the <u>slow, dull pace of life in Maycomb County</u>. The use of **nowhere, nothing** and **no** are used to emphasize this characteristic of the small town.

*"Well now, one winter it was so cold that all the **geese flew backward** and all the **fish moved south** and even the **snow turned blue**. Late at night, it got so frigid that all **spoken words froze solid** afore they could be heard. People had to wait until sunup to find out what folks were talking about the night before."*

_____
An excerpt from *Bunyan and Babe the Blue Ox* by Paul Bunyan

From the above excerpt, you can understand that the writer uses hyperbole to <u>emphasize how cold it is</u> in a comical way by using the underlined phrases.

EXERCISE 3

Can you make hyperboles using the following lines of dialogue?
1. Look at that incredible amount of snow piled up outside.
   The snow is so deep that_____
2. The weather feels incredibly hot today.
   It is so hot that _____

Similes

Most narratives or stories contain similes. These devices draw similarities between two unlike things. In other words, they say that something is similar to something else. Writers like to use similes to make their writings more interesting or prove a point.

Examples:

    a. Kate feels **as fresh as a daisy** today.

"As fresh as a daisy" is the simile in this sentence. You can infer that Kate feels healthy and full of energy on this particular day.

    b. Jackson **ran like the wind** to the candy store.

"Ran like the wind" is the simile in this sentence. You can infer that Jackson ran very fast to the candy store.

    c. Larry is as **good as gold** with that new job.

"Good as gold" is the simile in this sentence. You can infer that Larry is very competent in his new job.

> *The Tin Woodman was about to reply when he heard a low growl, and turning his head (which worked beautifully on hinges) he saw a strange beast come bounding over the grass toward them. It was, indeed, a great yellow Wildcat, and the Woodman thought it must be chasing something, for its ears were lying close to its head and its mouth was wide open, showing two rows of ugly teeth, while **its red eyes glowed like balls of fire**. As it came nearer, the Tin Woodman saw that running before the beast was a little gray field mouse, and although he had no heart, he knew it was wrong for the Wildcat to try to kill such a pretty, harmless creature.*

-An excerpt from *The Wonderful Wizard of Oz* by L. Frank Baum (1901)

From the excerpt above, the simile is "its red eyes glowed like balls of fire." You can infer that the Wildcat's eyes glowed a bright red color, which can be connected to its determination to catch the mouse.

Note: You can also create sentences using similes; for example, you can write many sentences using the simile "sleep like a baby."

a. Jenny *slept like a baby* after lunch.
b. After doing some Yoga, Andrew *slept like a baby* that night.
c. The cough medicine made him drowsy, and he *slept like a baby*.
d. Marcus had just gotten off a 24-hr shift at the hospital. When he reached home, he collapsed in bed and *slept like a baby*, waking up 10 hours later.

EXERCISE 4

1. Can you write a sentence using each of the following similes? Compare your answers with a partner's.

   a. "As quick as a cat" _____
   b. "As tough as nails" _____

2. What are the similes in the sentences below?

   a. My little brother swam like a fish in the ocean._____
   b. Amanda looked like an angel in that white dress. _____

Metaphors

These are often confused with similes. Metaphors make comparisons by saying that something *is* something else. They use words such as "is," "are" or "was." It is important to learn the meaning of metaphoric phrases so you can understand what you read, listen to and say in everyday life.

Examples:

1) Trevor tried to lift the barrel, but **his legs became wax.**

"His legs were wax" is the metaphor in this sentence. Trevor's legs are being compared to wax. You can infer that Trevor could not lift the barrel because he had weak legs.

2) Lala **swam in a sea of diamonds** when she got a perfect report card.

"Swam in a sea of diamonds" is the metaphor in this sentence. Here, Lala's joy is being compared to a sea of diamonds. You can infer that Lala's perfect report card made her happy and excited.

*Every **rose** has its thorn,*
Just like every night has it's dawn,
*Just like every cowboy sings his **sad, sad song**,*
Every rose has its thorn

_____

An excerpt from Poison's 1988 song "Every Rose Has Its Thorn"

From the excerpt above, Poison takes a popular metaphor and puts it into a song. Just like the flower so beautiful and beloved, the person's relationship has a side that can hurt. In the second metaphor, the heartbreak is comparable to that felt in traditional westerns.

EXERCISE 5

Read each sentence and underline the metaphor. Then, on the lines provided, write the two things being compared.

1) Reality is his worst enemy sometimes.

_____ is compared to _____

2) The principal's announcement of the holiday was music to the students' ears.

_____ is compared to _____

PRACTICE EXERCISES

1. Read the following passage and answer the questions. What do the underlined phrases mean?

On Friday night, my friends and I snuck out and went to the club. The following morning, **my feet were killing me!** My mum was furious, and as a punishment, she ordered me to clean out the garage or else she would take my phone away. All day long, I worked my **fingers to the bone**, getting things together so I could keep my phone. I was also **dying to see** the new movie at the cinema and hoped my mum would have calmed down by then. When I finished, however, **I was so tired that I couldn't move**.

a. "My feet were killing me" really means

_____

b. "Worked my fingers to the bone" really means

_____

c. "Dying to see" really means

_____

d. "I was so tired that I couldn't move" really means

_____

2. Read the following excerpt from *Touched by an Angel* by Maya Angelou (Date unknown):

> We, unaccustomed to courage
> exiles from delight
> live coiled in shells of loneliness
> until love leaves its high holy temple
> and comes into our sight
> to liberate us into life.
> Love arrives
> and in its train come ecstasies
> old memories of pleasure
> ancient histories of pain.
> Yet if we are bold,
> love strikes away the chains of fear
> from our souls.
> We are weaned from our timidity
> In the flush of love's light
> we dare be brave
> And suddenly we see
> that love costs all we are
> and will ever be.
> Yet it is only love
> which sets us free.

a. What comes to mind when you read the poem?

_____
_____
_____

b. Write down the instances of hyperbole that have been used.

_____
_____
_____

c. Write down the instances of alliteration that have been used.

_____
_____
_____

3. Below are sentences that contain either metaphors or similes. Identify which sentence has a metaphor and which has a simile.

a. The sky was the color of the calm Pacific, which was thousands of miles from land.

_____

b. My noisy sister was like a buzzing fly. _____

c. The child's tears were cold raindrops from a tiny cloud. _____

d. Like a silent thief, the dog crept into the kitchen. _____

4. Below is a paragraph about going to the grocery store. Rewrite the paragraph, adding hyperboles to the underlined phrases. Compare your answers with a partner's.

Lacy and her brother went to the market on Monday evening. While they were walking, it began to rain very hard. By the time they entered the door, they were quite wet. Lacy selected a shopping trolley, but its wheels were squeaky. They wobbled as she pushed it down the aisle. Her brother quickly selected the groceries on the list. Although they didn't have many items, the total was still a lot. They grabbed the bags of groceries, which were very heavy, and returned home.

_____

_____

_____

5. Read the following passage. Identify the symbol, and explain what you think it means. Work with a classmate.

Carol tried to concentrate on what Daniel was saying, but she was distracted when a small spider suddenly dropped from the ceiling and hung on a thread. He hung there in the air for a moment, swinging back and forth just over Daniels' left shoulder. Daniel continued to explain himself. Carol nodded, half-listening, as she watched the spider fasten one end of his thread to the door frame and set off once again through the air, beginning to build his web.

a. What is the symbol? _____

b. What do you think it might mean? _____

_____

REFLECTION ON LEARNING

Answer the following reflection questions, and feel free to discuss your responses with your teacher or classmate.

- What reading idea or strategy did you learn from this section?

- What new concepts did you learn?

- What methods did you work on in this section?

- What aspect of this section is still not 100 percent clear for you?

- What do you want your teacher to know?

LESSON 6

READING LONG PASSAGES

This lesson is vital to your progression in the lessons that follow. You will be asked to read long passages and extract answers from them. By the end of this lesson, you will have explored a few tips for reading long passages.

When reading a passage, use the following strategies.

BE PATIENT	Be patient with yourself, and go at a speed that works for you. An organic process that becomes part of your day-to-day life is vital. Before you know it, you'll be instinctively working towards improving your comprehension without knowing that you are. In exam situations, pay attention to the allocated time.
AVOID MEMORIZING	You should prioritize understanding the structure, the flow of information and the main ideas in a passage. You don't need to memorize each word; however, write down unfamiliar words and find their definition later. For questions that require factual or specific answers, you can always re-read the passage.
USE DIFFERENT QUESTION TYPES	Questions come in a variety of forms but fall under two main categories: multiple-choice or explanation questions. Familiarize yourself with different question types. The best way to do this is to do as many practice tests as you can.
READ QUESTIONS FIRST	If asked to find answers in a passage, read the questions carefully. Doing so will allow you to focus on the information that you need to find. In exam situations, this will help save time.
AVOID GETTING STUCK ON VOCABULARY WORDS	Avoid getting stuck on particular words and phrases. The best thing to do is mark these problematic words and keep reading. Try to get the gist of the passage first, then go back to these difficult words while looking for contextual cues and surrounding words that help identify their meanings.
ANSWERS ARE ALWAYS WITHIN THE PASSAGE (UNLESS OTHERWISE STATED)	Answers are always in the passage unless otherwise stated. That is to say, if asked to relate a passage to something external, some of the information needed is still within the text.
AVOID RELYING ON "TRIGGER" WORDS	Words like "but" and "however" are trigger words connecting different ideas. Pay attention to the main ideas presented in the text, and avoid rushing through necessary evidence and information to find these words.
FOCUS ON OPENING AND CLOSING PARAGRAPHS	Often, the main idea of a passage can be found in the opening and closing paragraphs. These paragraphs introduce and summarize the idea of the passage.
USE K-W-L CHARTS	You've probably heard about these charts in the previous manuals. These charts usually have three sections. At an advanced level, you instinctively apply these chart structures when reading. You may ask yourself: - What do I know about this topic? - What do I want to know? - What have I learned?
ON A FINAL NOTE: **THESE ARE USEFUL QUESTIONS TO ASK YOURSELF WHEN READING**	- What is the writer's main point? - Why did the writer write this? - How has the writer chosen to convey his main point? - How has the writer organized his material?

Let's break down a few things about passages, using possible questions that you may find in an exam. Read the following excerpt from *Jane Eyre* by Charlotte Bronte (1847):

"You need be in no hurry to hear," he said: "let me frankly tell you, I have nothing **eligible or profitable to suggest**. Before I explain, recall, if you please, my notice, clearly given, that if I helped you, it must be as the blind man would help the lame. I am **poor**; for I find that, when I have paid my father's debts, all the patrimony remaining to me will be this crumbling grange, the row of scathed firs behind, and the patch of moorish soil, with the yew-trees and holly-bushes in front. **I am obscure**: Rivers is an old name; but of the three sole descendants of the race, two earn the dependent's crust among strangers, and the third considers himself an alien from his native country—not only for life, but in death. Yes, and deems, and is bound to deem, himself honored by the lot, and aspires but after the day when the cross of separation from fleshly ties shall be laid on his shoulders, and when the Head of that church-militant of whose humblest members he is one, shall give the word, 'Rise, follow Me!'"

St. John said these words as he pronounced his sermons, with a quiet, deep voice; with an unflushed cheek, and a coruscating radiance of glance. He resumed—

"And since I am myself **poor and obscure**, I can offer you but a service of poverty and obscurity. You may even think it degrading—for I see now your habits have been what the world calls refined: your tastes lean to the ideal, and your society has at least been amongst the educated; but I consider that no service degrades which can better our race. I hold that the more arid and unreclaimed the soil **where the Christian laborer's task of tillage is appointed him—the scantier the meed his toil brings—the higher the honor**. His, under such circumstances, is the destiny of the pioneer; and the first pioneers of the Gospel were the Apostles—their captain was Jesus, the Redeemer, Himself."

1. **Identify the keywords/phrases.** The first step in gaining an understanding of the main idea in a long passage is to mark the keywords and phrases – these are in bold.

2. **PART A**

   Which of the following statements match the content in the passage?

   a. St. John speaks about his servitude to God.
   b. St. John berates crowds of people.
   c. St. John begs on the street for money.
   d. St. John rebukes Christianity.

   PART B

   Which sentence from the passage supports the answer to PART A?

   a. I am obscure: Rivers is an old name; but of the three sole descendants of the race, two earn the dependent's crust among strangers, and the third considers himself an alien from his native country—not only for life, but in death.

   b. I hold that the more arid and unreclaimed the soil where the Christian laborer's task of tillage is appointed him—the scantier the meed his toil brings—the higher the honor.

   c. You may even think it degrading—for I see now your habits have been what the world calls refined: your tastes lean to the ideal, and your society has at least been amongst the educated; but I consider that no service degrades which can better our race.

    d. "You need be in no hurry to hear," he said: "let me frankly tell you, I have nothing eligible or profitable to suggest."

The most suitable sentence that summarizes St John's sermon is b. This can be found towards the end of the passage and matches the title.

3. **PART A**

Identify the main <u>idea</u>.

    a. You have to be poor to be a Christian.

    b. **St. John's sermon is to convince the other characters to join him in servitude.**

    c. St. John hates the crowd of listeners.

    d. St. John's sermon is to detract the other characters from joining him in his servitude.

The most suitable answer is b. You can infer the passage is about St. John. He seems to be preaching and trying to convince the other characters of the benefits of servitude in Christianity.

PART B

Why did you choose this option? (You can use a text-to-world connection to answer this question.)

    a. Because St. John's existence doesn't mean anything

    b. Because sermons are meant to incite a rebellion

    c. Because St. John seems determined to oust himself from the community

    d. **Because sermons are meant to deliver a specific message to the listeners**

PRACTICE EXERCISE

Passage 1

You are about to read a passage by Virginia B. Spivey based on Pablo Picasso's painting *Guernica*. The title of the passage is **Pablo Picasso's *Guernica* and Modern War.** The following is the introductory paragraph:

> *First shown at the 1937 International Exposition in Paris, Guernica stands today as a universal statement against the horror of modern warfare. The painting was the response of the Spanish-born artist, Pablo Picasso, to the bombing of Guernica, a small Basque town in northern Spain that was destroyed on April 26, 1937, during the Spanish Civil War.*

Fill in the first two sections of the K-W-L chart.

WHAT DO I KNOW ABOUT THIS TOPIC? (HERE, WRITE DOWN ANY BACKGROUND KNOWLEDGE)	WHAT DO I WANT TO KNOW?

Continue reading the passage and answer the following questions:

Picasso initially rejected the invitation to represent his native country in the prestigious exhibition. Spain was embroiled in a bloody Civil War. In 1936, Nationalist forces, supported by the military and groups loyal to the Spanish monarchy, rebelled against a new Republican government, which was founded on the democratic and communist principles of Spain's working classes. Nationalist General Francisco Franco, who became Spain's dictator in 1939 until his death in 1975, allied himself with fascist governments in Italy and Germany to take advantage of their powerful industrialized militaries.

Picasso's change of heart reflected the international public outcry that followed the bombing of Guernica. The attack was one of the first demonstrations of a full-scale aerial bombardment. Carried out by the German Luftwaffe's Condor Legion and the Italian Aviazione Legionaria, the three-hour raid left the ancient town in ruins and many children among the civilian dead. Guernica served as a frightening show of Germany's military might and an intentional warning to other nations in the years before World War II.

Picasso's painting, however, includes no obvious references to the Guernica bombing or the Spanish Civil War. The mammoth eleven-foot by twenty-five-foot canvas is a synthesis of modern painting styles. Picasso's compressed pictorial space and fragmented forms are characteristic of Cubism. The heightened emotion and disjointed imagery reflect Surrealism's interest in the workings of the inner mind, imagined through dreams, or in this case, nightmares. The monochromatic color scheme recalls Cubism, but also the black and white newspapers that broadcast the devastating effects of the bombing around the world. Captured clearly in photographs and newsreels, images of the bombing's aftermath altered people's perceptions of modern war, its toll on individuals, and its essential inhumanity.

1. **PART A**

   In this passage, the name *Guernica* refers to two things. What are they?

   _____

   _____

   PART B.

   What is the evidence for the answers you have given in Part A?

   _____

   _____

2. Which of the following statement(s) are true? (Choose all that apply and provide evidence for your choices)

    a. General Francisco Franco retaliated against Germany and Italy following the bombings.
    b. Picasso's painting was a response based on the bombing of *Guernica*.
    c. An example of Cubism painting technique is using a compressed pictorial space.
    d. The bombing of Guernica happened after World War II.

_____

_____

3. When was *Guernica* destroyed?

    a. April 26, 1937
    b. April 26, 1927
    c. January 26, 1936
    d. April 16, 1937

4. **PART A**

Who did not take part in the attack against *Guernica*?

    a. German Luftwaffe's Condor Legion
    b. Italian Aviazione Legionaria
    c. José Canalejas
    d. General Francisco Franco

PART B

Who took advantage of the situation and allied themselves with fascist governments to destroy *Guernica?*

    a. German Luftwaffe's Condor Legion
    b. Italian Aviazione Legionaria
    c. José Canalejas
    d. General Francisco Franco

5. **PART A.**

What is the main idea in the passage above?

_____

_____

PART B.

Provide three examples as your evidence.

_____

_____

_____

6. What are the two modern painting styles that Picasso used? Compare your answer with a partner's.

_____

_____

7. Fill out the last section of the K-W-L chart and discuss your response with a classmate.

WHAT HAVE I LEARNED?

Passage 2

You are about to read a passage based on Charles Darwin's travels on board the *HMS Beagle* as a naturalist. These writings were based on his observations as the ship traveled the waters of South America. They were later published as *The Voyager of the Beagle (1839)*.

Fill in the first two sections of the K-W-L chart.

WHAT DO I KNOW ABOUT THIS TOPIC? (HERE, WRITE DOWN ANY BACKGROUND KNOWLEDGE I.E., WHAT DO YOU KNOW ABOUT CHARLES DARWIN?)	WHAT DO I WANT TO KNOW?

Read this passage to answer the questions below:

I have not as yet noticed by far the most remarkable feature in the natural history of this archipelago; it is, that the different islands to a considerable extent are inhabited by a different set of beings. My attention was first called to this fact by the Vice-Governor, Mr. Lawson, declaring that the tortoises differed from the different islands, and that he could with certainty tell from which island any one was brought. I did not for some time pay sufficient attention to this statement, and I had already partially mingled together the collections from two of the islands. I never dreamed that islands, about 50 or 60 miles apart, and most of them in sight of each other, formed of precisely the same rocks, placed under a quite similar climate, rising to a nearly equal height, would have been differently tenanted; but we shall soon see that this is the case. It is the fate of most voyagers, no sooner to discover what is most interesting in any locality, than they are hurried from it; but I ought, perhaps, to be thankful that I obtained sufficient materials to establish this most remarkable fact in the distribution of organic beings.

The inhabitants, as I have said, state that they can distinguish the tortoises from the different islands; and that they differ not only in size, but in other characters. Captain Porter has described 175 those from Charles and from the nearest island to it, namely, Hood Island, as having their shells in front thick and turned up like a Spanish saddle, whilst the tortoises from James Island are rounder, blacker, and have a better taste when cooked. M. Bibron, moreover, informs me that he has seen what he considers two distinct species of tortoise from the Galapagos, but he does not know from which islands. The specimens that I brought from three islands were young ones: and probably owing to this cause neither Mr. Gray nor myself could find in them any specific differences. I have remarked that the marine Amblyrhynchus was larger at Albemarle Island than elsewhere; and M. Bibron informs me that he has seen two distinct aquatic species of this genus; so that the different islands probably have their representative species or races of the Amblyrhynchus, as well as of the tortoise. My attention was first <u>thoroughly aroused</u>, by comparing together the numerous specimens, shot by myself and several other parties on board, of the mocking-thrushes, when, to my astonishment, I discovered that all those from Charles Island belonged to one species (Mimus trifasciatus) all from Albemarle Island to M. parvulus; and all from James and Chatham Islands (between which two other islands are situated, as connecting links) belonged to M. melanotis. These two latter species are closely allied, and would by some ornithologists be considered as only well-marked races or varieties; but the Mimus trifasciatus is very distinct. Unfortunately most of the specimens of the finch tribe were mingled together; but I have strong reasons to suspect that some of the species of the sub-group Geospiza are confined to separate islands. If the different islands have their representatives of Geospiza, it may help to explain the <u>singularly</u> large number of the species of this sub-group in this one small archipelago, and as a probable consequence of their numbers, the perfectly graduated series in the size of their beaks. Two species of the sub-group Cactornis, and two of the Camarhynchus, were procured in the archipelago; and of the numerous specimens of these two sub-groups shot by four collectors at James Island, all were found to belong to one species of each; whereas the numerous specimens shot either on Chatham or Charles Island (for the two sets were mingled together) all belonged to the two other species: hence we may feel almost sure that these islands possess their respective species of these two sub-groups. In land-shells this law of distribution does not appear to hold good. In my very small collection of insects, Mr. Waterhouse remarks, that of those which were ticketed with their locality, not one was common to any two of the islands.

1. Break down each of the following words by separating the noun from the suffix.

    a. *Certainty:* _____

    b. *Precisely:* _____

    c. *Locality:* _____

    d. *Singularly:* _____

2. What is "the most remarkable feature in the natural history of this archipelago?"

    _____

3. What was the first animal in which this feature was seen by Mr. Lawson?

    _____

4. What is the main idea in this passage?

_____

_____

5. How did Darwin first take Mr. Lawson's observation?

_____

6. Why did Darwin think that he and Mr. Gray could not find any specific differences in the specimens that were brought back from the Galapagos?

_____

_____

7. When was Darwin's attention to the differences in species between the islands "first thoroughly aroused?"

_____

8. The specimens of what "tribe" were mingled together?

_____

9. Fill out the last section of the K-W-L chart.

WHAT HAVE I LEARNT

REFLECTION ON LEARNING

Answer the following reflection questions, and feel free to discuss your responses with your teacher or classmate.

- What reading idea or strategy did you learn from this section?

- What new concepts did you learn?

- What methods did you work on in this section?

- What aspect of this section is still not 100 percent clear for you?

- What do you want your teacher to know?

LESSON 7

MINI-PRACTICE TEST

You have reached the midway point of this manual. Complete the following mini-practice test to gauge whether you have understood what you have read so far. Feel free to go back to the lessons to refresh your mind.

1. PART A

"It took a million years for Thomas to finish his homework." This line is an example of what? **(See Lesson 5.)**

   a. Simile
   b. Hyperbole
   c. Personification
   d. Onomatopoeia

   PART B

   Can you rewrite the sentence but retain the same meaning?

   _____

2. PART A

   "Lucky lady" is an example of what? **(See Lesson 5.)**

   a. Metaphor
   b. Oxymoron
   c. Hyperbole
   d. Alliteration

   Can you rewrite the phrase but retain the same meaning?

   _____

Read the following excerpt from *Around the World in Eighty Days* by Jules Verne (1873).

> *"I know it; I don't blame you. We start for Dover and Calais in ten minutes."*
>
> *A puzzled grin <u>overspread</u> Passepartout's round face; clearly he had not comprehended his master.*
>
> *"Monsieur is going to leave home?"*
>
> *"Yes," <u>returned</u> Phileas Fogg. "We are going round the world."*
>
> *Passepartout opened wide his eyes, raised his eyebrows, held up his hands, and seemed about to collapse, so overcome was he with stupefied astonishment.*
>
> *"Round the world!" he murmured.*
>
> *"In eighty days," responded Mr. Fogg. "So we haven't a moment to lose."*
>
> *"But the trunks?" gasped Passepartout, unconsciously swaying his head from right to left.*

"We'll have no trunks; only a <u>carpet-bag</u>, with two shirts and three pairs of stockings for me, and the same for you. We'll buy our clothes on the way. Bring down my <u>mackintosh</u> and traveling-cloak, and some <u>stout</u> shoes, though we shall do little walking. Make haste!"

Passepartout tried to reply, but could not. He went out, mounted to his own room, fell into a chair, and muttered: "That's good, that is! And I, who wanted to remain quiet!"

He mechanically set about making the preparations for departure. Around the world in eighty days! Was his master a fool? No. Was this a joke, then? They were going to Dover; good! To Calais; good again! After all, Passepartout, who had been away from France five years, would not be sorry to set foot on his <u>native</u> soil again. Perhaps they would go as far as Paris, and it would do his eyes good to see Paris once more. But surely a gentleman so <u>chary</u> of his steps would stop there; no doubt—but, then, it was none the less true that he was going away, this so domestic person <u>hitherto</u>!

By eight o'clock, Passepartout had packed the modest carpet-bag, containing the <u>wardrobes</u> of his master and himself; then, still troubled in mind, he carefully shut the door of his room, and descended to Mr. Fogg.

3. What do you think the underlined words mean? **(See Lesson 2.)**

   a) *overspread:* _____

   b) *returned:* _____

   c) *carpet-bag:* _____

   d) *mackintosh:* _____

   e) *stout:* _____

   f) *native:* _____

   g) *chary:* _____

   h) *hitherto:* _____

   i) *wardrobes:* _____

4. **PART A**

   In your words, what kind of man is *Mr. Fogg?*

   _____

   PART B

   Provide evidence based on the excerpt above.

   _____

   _____

   _____

5. Does *Passepartout* miss being home? Provide evidence to support your answer.

_____

_____

Read the following excerpt from *Peter Pan* by James M. Barrie (1902).

All children, except one, grow up. They soon know that they will grow up, and the way Wendy knew was this. One day when she was two years old, she was playing in a garden, and she plucked another flower and ran with it to her mother. I suppose she must have looked rather delightful, for Mrs. Darling put her hand to her heart and cried, "Oh, why can't you remain like this for ever!" This was all that passed between them on the subject, but henceforth Wendy knew that she must grow up. You always know after you are two. Two is the beginning of the end.

Of course, they lived at 14 [their house number on their street], and until Wendy came, her mother was the chief one. She was a lovely lady, with a romantic mind and such a sweet mocking mouth. Her romantic mind was like the tiny boxes, one within the other, that come from the puzzling East, however many you discover there is always one more; and her sweet mocking mouth had one kiss on it that Wendy could never get, though there it was, perfectly <u>conspicuous</u> in the right-hand corner.

The way Mr. Darling won her was this: the many gentlemen who had been boys when she was a girl discovered simultaneously that they loved her, and they all ran to her house to propose to her except Mr. Darling, who took a cab and nipped in first, and so he got her. He got all of her, except the innermost box and the kiss. He never knew about the box, and in time he gave up trying for the kiss. Wendy thought Napoleon could have got it, but I can picture him trying, and then going off in a passion, slamming the door.

6. **PART A**

   From the passage, what can you infer about Mrs. Darling?

   a. She is indecisive.
   b. She unintentionally refuses those around her
   c. She has a chaotic marriage.
   d. She is an assertive, complex woman.
   e. She is artistic and fickle-minded.

   PART B

   Give evidence to support your answer.

   _____

   _____

7. What does the writer's description of Mrs. Darling's "sweet mocking mouth" indicate?

   a. Mrs. Darling often ridicules others.
   b. Mrs. Darling is like a mockingbird that mimics others and sings sweet songs.
   c. Mrs. Darling is loving but does not give away all her love.
   d. Mrs. Darling speaks lovingly to her children but often insults her husband.
   e. Mrs. Darling has a scarred mouth.

8. The word "conspicuous" is underlined. What does it mean in this context? Provide evidence.

_____

_____

9. **PART A**

What is the main idea of the passage above?

_____

_____

PART B

Provide three examples as your evidence.

_____

_____

_____

10.   Choose a connector from the parenthesis to fill in each gap. **(See Lesson 3.)**

a. **(due to, but to, so)** Jade feels like she could be sick, _____ she asks her mother to take her to the hospital. On their way to the hospital, the car tire bursts _____ _____a stray nail on the road. They have no option _____ _____ call an ambulance.

b. **(both, but, that)** Alan refers to himself as a comedian _____ he is not funny. He makes crude jokes _____ most people do not like. _____ his brother and wife have asked him to choose another career.

11.   Break down each word and give the root word, prefix/suffix and meaning.
    (See Lesson 2.)

WORD	PREFIX	ROOT WORD	SUFFIX	MEANING
Fertility				
Physician				
Superficial				
Nonsense				
Intermission				

12.   Read the following sentence. **(See Lesson 5.)**

Tanya's thoughts fluttered from subject to subject like a butterfly visiting flowers in a field.

Does it have a metaphor or simile?_____

REFLECTION ON LEARNING

Answer the following reflection questions, and feel free to discuss your responses with your teacher or classmate.

- What reading idea or strategy did you learn from this section?

- What new concepts did you learn?

- What methods did you work on in this section?

- What aspect of this section is still not 100 percent clear for you?

- What do you want your teacher to know?

LESSON 8

UNDERSTANDING MAIN IDEAS AND FINDING EVIDENCE

By the end of this lesson, you will learn a few techniques to help you understand a text's main idea and use evidence to back up your conclusions. A main idea is a sentence that sums up the most important message or information in a passage. It is tied to the theme of the text. The main idea can also be the central idea of a section, a paragraph or the entire text.

1. Example

"Mum, can I have a puppy?" Lanny pleaded with her dad.

"I'm not sure you can handle a puppy right now, Lanny. You have school and Jackle, your pet parrot, to take care of," her dad said.

"Please, please. I promise I can take care of the puppy and the parrot and do well in school too!" Lanny cried.

Lanny did all she could to prove to her dad that she could take care of everything. She got up early every morning, fed the parrot, and did some pre-school reading. In the evenings, she would finish her homework accurately and on time and clean out the parrot cage.

From the above example, you can infer the main idea of the passage: Lanny does all she can to prove to her dad that she can take on the responsibility of caring for a puppy as he believes she has enough responsibilities.

2. Example

Before the farmer disposes of his cotton, or rather, before he is willing to dispose of it, it has to be put in marketable shape in the form of a bale, and prior to bailing, has to be ginned. The seed cotton is attached to these by one end of each fiber, just as the human hair is attached to the head. To remove the fiber from the seed, the gin used in America, except for Sea Island cotton, is generally of the variety known as the saw gin, and after the lint has been removed, it is baled in the baling press.

(An excerpt from *Cotton: Its Uses, Varieties, Fiber structure, Cultivation, and Preparation for the Market*, Christopher Brooks)

From the above example, you can infer that the main idea of the passage explains the ginning and bailing stage of cotton harvesting.

PRACTICE EXERCISES

1. In your own words, can you state the main idea of the following passage?

A great part of what Edison has done is now so much a part of our lives and so commonplace that we forget we owe it to him. His work has not only created many millions of new jobs but also, and without qualification, it has made every job more remunerative. Edison has done more toward abolishing poverty than have all the reformers and statesmen since the beginning of the world. He has provided man with the means to help himself. The work of Edison falls into two great divisions. The first has to do with his direct contributions of inventions of tools. The second has to do with his example in linking science with our everyday life and demonstrating that, through patient, unremitting testing and trying, any problem may eventually be solved. It is certainly useless and probably impossible to determine whether his actual accomplishments or the force of his example has been the more valuable to us.

An excerpt from *Edison as I know Him* by Henry Ford (1930)

Read the following passage and ask yourself, "What is the author trying to tell me?"

> The expression of his face as he said these words was not at all pleasant, and I had my own reasons for thinking that the stranger was mistaken, even supposing he meant what he said. But it was no affair of mine, I thought; and besides, it was difficult to know what to do. The stranger kept hanging about just inside the inn door, peering round the corner like a cat waiting for a mouse. Once I stepped out myself into the road, but he immediately called me back, and as I did not obey quick enough for his fancy, a most horrible change came over his tallowy face, and he ordered me in with an oath that made me jump. As soon as I was back again he returned to his former manner, half fawning, half sneering, patted me on the shoulder, told me I was a good boy and he had taken quite a fancy to me.
>
> -An excerpt from *Treasure Island* by Robert Louis Stevenson (1883)

2. **PART A**

What is the main idea in this paragraph?

_____

_____

_____

Part B

What is your evidence?

_____

_____

3. Suggest an appropriate title for the paragraph.

_____

Read the following poem: *Summer Night* by Alfred Tennyson (1890).

> Now sleeps the crimson petal, now the white;
> Nor waves the cypress in the palace walk;
> Nor winks the gold fin in the porphyry font:
> The firefly wakens: waken thou with me.
> Now droops the milk-white peacock like a ghost,
> And like a ghost she glimmers on to me.
> Now lies the Earth all Danaë to the stars,
> And all thy heart lies open unto me.
> Now slides the silent meteor on, and leaves
> A shining furrow, as thy thoughts in me.
> Now folds the lily all her sweetness up,
> And slips into the bosom of the lake.
> So fold thyself, my dearest, thou, and slip
> Into my bosom and be lost in me.

4. **PART A**

   What is the main idea in this poem? Discuss your answer with a classmate.

   _____

   _____

   _____

   PART B

   What is your evidence? Compare your answer with a classmate's.

   _____

   _____

   _____

5. Suggest an appropriate title other than the current one.

   _____

Look at the image below before answering questions about it.

6. What does the image tell you?

   _____

   _____

7. In a few words, write text to accompany this image.

   _____

   _____

8. Can you suggest a title?

   _____

Look at the image below.

The Text of an Eyewitness Account of the Trinity Bomb Test, 1945

I was kneeling between the pilot and co-pilot in B-29 No. 384 and observed the explosion through the pilot's window on the left side of the plane. We were about 20 to 25 miles from the site and the cloud cover between us and the ground was approximately 7/10. About 30 seconds before the object was detonated, the clouds obscured our vision of the point so that we did not see glasses directly at the site. My first sensation was one of intense light covering my whole field of vision.

(Sourced from https://dp.la/primary-source-sets/the-atomic-bomb-and-the-nuclear-age/sources/51)

9. Complete the following K-W-L chart:

WHAT DID I KNOW ABOUT THIS TOPIC?	WHAT DID I WANT TO KNOW?	WHAT HAVE I LEARNT?

10. What can you infer from the image, text and title provided above?

_____

_____

_____

11. What is the main idea connecting the image, title and text?

_____

_____

_____

12. Suggest an appropriate title other than the current one.

_____

REFLECTION ON LEARNING

Answer the following reflection questions, and feel free to discuss your responses with your teacher or classmate.

- What reading idea or strategy did you learn from this section?

- What new concepts did you learn?

- What methods did you work on in this section?

- What aspect of this section is still not 100 percent clear for you?

- What do you want your teacher to know?

LESSON 9

MAKING INFERENCES AND PREDICTIONS

Sometimes, writers imply themes and ideas without stating them outright. Therefore, it is important for readers to be able to make inferences or conclusions when reading. By the end of this lesson, you will learn how to use different techniques to make inferences and predictions based on the written material provided to you. We will concentrate on direct/indirect characterization, drawing conclusions, and character descriptions.

Direct/Indirect Characterization

Characterization is an important element in every work of fiction, and sometimes non-fiction, whether it is a short story, a novel or a biography.

Direct characterization involves making direct statements about a character's personality and showing the reader what the character is like.

Indirect characterization involves the writer revealing information about a character and their personality through that character's thoughts, words and actions. Information is also revealed in other characters' responses to that character, including what they think and say about the character or person.

Examples of Characterization

Direct: Anna is rich.
Indirect: Anna wore a twelve-carat diamond ring everywhere she went.

Direct: Donna and Mark were having fun at the party.
Indirect: Neither Donna nor Mark could believe it was 5 in the morning, but they didn't want to leave yet.

Direct: Sally is socially awkward.
Indirect: All Sally does when people are around is say weird things that nobody understands.

A Small Task
Exercise 1

Rewrite the following direct characterization examples as indirect characterizations.

1. Direct: He smells good.
   Indirect: _____

2. Direct: Sonya is very smart.
   Indirect: _____

Rewrite the following indirect characterization examples as a direct characterization.

3. Indirect: The man's clothes were filthy, probably since he'd been sleeping on newspapers all night.
   Direct: _____

4. Indirect: When she heard her baby crying last night, she gritted her teeth and turned up her iPod.
   Direct: _____

Drawing Conclusions and Making Predictions

Learning to draw conclusions and inferences develops over time and requires you to put together various pieces of information. Making predictions can be a hit or miss, but this is where text-to-self and text-to-world connections come in. This skill relies on good word knowledge.

> *As I walked through the door, I was amazed at the <u>beautiful colors and smells</u>. I knew it would be hard to decide what to buy with my $3. <u>The chocolate truffles</u> looked delicious, but they were expensive. The <u>jelly beans</u> were not only cheaper but so colorful! With so much to choose from, I knew I would be here a long time.*

From the above example, you can infer that the scenario is happening in a candy store. The underlined words are your evidence. You understand that the character has walked into a room that contains sweets. You can also predict, and make a *text-to-self connection*, that the character will be in the store for a while, browsing through the selection of sweets.

> *It felt wonderful to be <u>outside</u>, even if only for a little while! All the <u>swings</u> were already taken, and a group <u>played softball</u> on the diamond. Casey and I decided to use the <u>monkey bars</u> until the teacher called us.*

From the above example, you can infer that the scenario is happening in a playground. The underlined words are your evidence. You understand that the character is outside playing with their friend, Casey. You can also predict that once the teacher calls them, they'll have to return to class.

From the above picture, you can infer that the man is a chef based on the following evidence:
(a) He is surrounded by crockery and cutlery found in a restaurant
(b) He seems to be measuring something into a cup. You can predict that the chef is making a meal for a customer or getting ready before opening his restaurant.

EXERCISE 2

Read the following passage.

I was allowed to push the cart. The front left wheel was broken, so the cart wobbled down each aisle. Mother put various packages and boxes in the cart, but I didn't notice. I was trying to keep the cart rolling straight as it got heavier and heavier.

1. **PART A**

   Where did this scenario occur? _____

   PART B
   Explain your answer.

   _____
   _____

2. What are two predictions you can extract from the text?

   _____
   _____

3. What can you infer from this picture?

   _____

   _____

   _____

Character Descriptions

Visual descriptions help readers "see" characters when they are in action; the more descriptive, the better the imagery. Readers can make conclusions about a character's gender, occupation and personality traits based on clues in the text.

I had finally gotten used to being <u>weightless</u>. It became a comfortable feeling. I especially <u>liked floating by the window to see Earth below</u>.

From the above example, you can understand that the character is an <u>astronaut</u>. The underlined words/phrases are evidence.

Tom sat by his desk pondering. His mind was restless. He was <u>ridden with guilt and ashamed</u> at what he had done. He had no other option but to <u>turn himself in</u>. He stood up and walked out of his apartment. He was determined to make things right.

From the above example, you can understand that the character has <u>done something horrible</u>. He was feeling guilty and needed to make things right. You understand that he is taking responsibility for his actions. You can also infer that he would be turning himself in to the police. This increases the magnitude of what he had done. The underlined words/phrases in the reading are the evidence.

John Reed was a schoolboy of fourteen years old; four years older than I, for I was but ten: large and stout for his age, with a dingy and unwholesome skin; thick lineaments in a spacious visage, heavy limbs and large extremities. He gorged himself habitually at table, which made him bilious, and gave him a dim and bleared eye and flabby cheeks. He ought now to have been at school; but his mama had taken him home for a month or two, "on account of his delicate health." Mr. Miles, the master, affirmed that he would do very well if he had fewer cakes and sweetmeats sent him from home; but the mother's heart turned from an opinion so harsh, and inclined rather to the more refined idea that John's sallowness was owing to over-application and, perhaps, to pining after home. John had not much affection for his mother and sisters, and an antipathy to me. He bullied and punished me; not two or three times in the week, nor once or twice in the day, but continually: every nerve I had feared him, and every morsel of flesh in my bones shrank when he came near. There were moments when I was bewildered by the terror he inspired, because I had no appeal whatever against either his menaces or his inflictions; the servants did not like to offend their young master by taking my part against him, and Mrs. Reed was blind and deaf on the subject: she never saw him strike or heard him abuse me, though he did both now and then in her very presence, more frequently, however, behind her back. Habitually obedient to John, I came up to his chair: he spent some three minutes in thrusting out his tongue at me as far as he could without damaging the roots: I knew he would soon strike, and while dreading the blow, I mused on the disgusting and ugly appearance of him who would presently deal it. I wonder if he read that notion in my face; for, all at once, without speaking, he struck suddenly and strongly. I tottered, and on regaining my equilibrium retired back a step or two from his chair.

-An excerpt from *Jane Eyre* by Charlotte Bronte (1847)

From the above extensive example, you can extract some character traits about John Reed. The underlined words give you a clue as to what they are. You can infer that John Reed is **greedy** from the statement "gorged himself" and the reference to his body size. You can also infer that John is **spoiled** due to his mother's reaction to being told about his bad behavior.

EXERCISE 3

1. Can you list two other character traits? Explain your answers.

_____

_____

2. The character's POV is Jane. Describe two of Jane's character traits that are different from John's.

_____

_____

PRACTICE EXERCISES

Read the following excerpt from _The Adventures of Tom Sawyer_ by Mark Twain (1876) and answer the following questions:

Huckleberry was cordially hated and dreaded by all the mothers of the town, because he was idle and lawless and vulgar and bad—and because all their children admired him so, and delighted in his forbidden society, and wished they dared to be like him. Tom was like the rest of the respectable boys, in that he envied Huckleberry his gaudy outcast condition, and was under strict orders not to play with him. So, he played with him every time he got a chance. Huckleberry was always dressed in the cast-off clothes of full-grown men, and they were in perennial bloom and fluttering with rags. His hat was a vast ruin with a wide crescent lopped out of its brim; his coat, when he wore one, hung nearly to his heels and had the rearward buttons far down the back; but one suspender supported his trousers; the seat of the trousers bagged low and contained nothing, the fringed legs dragged in the dirt when not rolled up. Huckleberry came and went, at his own free will. He slept on doorsteps in fine weather and in empty hogsheads in wet; he did not have to go to school or to church, or call any being master or obey anybody; he could go fishing or swimming when and where he chose, and stay as long as it suited him; nobody forbade him to fight; he could sit up as late as he pleased; he was always the first boy that went barefoot in the spring and the last to resume leather in the fall; he never had to wash, nor put on clean clothes; he could swear wonderfully. In a word, everything that goes to make life precious that boy had. So thought every harassed, hampered, respectable boy in St. Petersburg.

1. Where did Huck's clothes come from?

_____

2. How did Huck hold up his pants?

_____

3. How often did Huck have to take a bath?

_____

4. Who told Huck what to do?

_____

5. When did Huck go barefoot?

Read the passage below and answer the following questions:

She was exactly like a child. She wanted to be with me always. She tried to follow me everywhere, and on my next journey out and about, it went to my heart to tire her down, and leave her at last, exhausted and calling after me rather plaintively. But the problems of the world had to be mastered. I had not, I said to myself, come into the future to carry on a miniature flirtation. Yet her distress when I left her was very great, her expostulations at the parting were sometimes frantic, and I think, altogether, I had as much trouble as comfort from her devotion. Nevertheless, she was, somehow, a very great comfort. I thought it was mere childish affection that made her cling to me. Until it was too late, I did not clearly know what I had inflicted upon her when I left her. Nor until it was too late did I clearly understand what she was to me. For, by merely seeming fond of me, and showing in her weak, futile way that she cared for me, the little doll of a creature presently gave my return to the neighborhood of the White Sphinx almost the feeling of coming home; and I would watch for her tiny figure of white and gold so soon as I came over the hill.

_____

An excerpt from _The Time Machine_ by H.G Wells (1895)

6. **PART A**

List five character traits of Weena, the female character the narrator is describing.

_____

_____

_____

_____

PART B

Write down your evidence.

_____

_____

_____

7. **PART A**

What two character traits of the Time Traveler are revealed in his description of Weena?

_____

_____

PART B

What is your evidence?

_____

_____

REFLECTION ON LEARNING

Answer the following reflection questions, and feel free to discuss your responses with your teacher or classmate.

- What reading idea or strategy did you learn from this section?

- What new concepts did you learn?

- What methods did you work on in this section?

- What aspect of this section is still not 100 percent clear for you?

- What do you want your teacher to know?

LESSON 10
CONSTRUCTING VISUAL IMAGERY

By the end of this lesson, you will learn how to use different techniques to construct visual imagery based on your reading. Writers often use descriptive language that allows readers to visualize characters and settings. This descriptive language allows readers to immerse themselves within the text and "see" what the writer is describing. In this lesson, we will look at <u>imagery in song lyrics</u>, <u>poems</u> and <u>literary nonfiction</u>.

Imagery in Song Lyrics

Think about your favorite song. Think about why you love that song so much and play it repeatedly without getting bored. Most often, you connect with the song, and even though there may not be many words, the song promotes a particular message you can infer based on the description.

Read the following song lyrics.

> Do you know that there's still a chance for you
> 'Cause there's a spark in you
> You just gotta ignite the light
> And let it shine
> Just own the night
> Like the Fourth of July
> Cause baby you're a firework
> Come on show 'em what your worth
> Make 'em go, "Oh, oh, oh!"
> As you shoot across the sky
> Baby, you're a firework
> Come on let your colors burst
> Make 'em go, "Oh, oh, oh!"
> You're gonna leave 'em all in awe, awe, awe
>
> An excerpt from "Fireworks" by Katy Perry (2009)

These lyrics create vivid imagery. At some point in your life, you may have been to a fireworks display or seen one in movies. The euphoria you feel while seeing the fireworks shoot to the sky and explode is linked to the message of the song. The song is a metaphor; it talks about the importance of revealing your true self, not being afraid to express what's inside you, and having pride in who you are and what you stand for.

What do you think about the song? Discuss your thoughts with a classmate.

_____

_____

_____

EXERCISE 1

1. Describe the visual imagery you get when you read the following lyrics from *"Wrecking Ball"* by Miley Cyrus (2013):

> *I came in like a wrecking ball*
> *I never hit so hard in love*
> *All I wanted was to break your walls*
> *All you ever did was wreck me*
> *Yeah, you wreck me*

_____

_____

2. What do you think the song is about? Discuss with a classmate.

_____

Imagery in Poems

Writers may rely on strong sensory details that give readers and listeners clear images of what they are trying to express. Poets are known for imbuing their poems with imagery so the reader can visualize the words.

Examples

Much I marveled this ungainly fowl to hear discourse so plainly,
Though its answer little meaning- little relevancy bore;
For we cannot help agreeing that no living human being
Ever yet was blest with seeing bird above his chamber door-
Bird or beast upon the sculptured bust above his chamber door,
With such name as "Nevermore."

But the raven, sitting lonely on the placid bust, spoke only
That one word, as if his soul in that one word he did outpour.
Nothing further then he uttered- not a feather then he fluttered-
Till I scarcely more than muttered, "other friends have flown before-
On the morrow he will leave me, as my hopes have flown before."
Then the bird said, "Nevermore."

———
An excerpt from *The Raven* by Edgar Allan Poe (1845)

From the example above, we can visualize the character looking at a bird that has perched itself on his door. Unlike a normal bird that would probably fly around the room scared, the raven sits on a statue of Athena, the goddess of wisdom, above the door. Rather unnaturally, the narrator begins to talk to it, asking for its name. And while you wouldn't expect a raven to be able to answer, he does respond with "Nevermore."

Did you hear about the rose that grew
from a crack in the concrete?
Proving nature's law is wrong it
learned to walk without having feet.
Funny it seems, but by keeping its dreams,
it learned to breathe fresh air.
Long live the rose that grew from concrete
when no one else ever cared.

The Rose That Grew from Concrete by Tupac Shakur
(1999)

From the example above, even though it is impossible, we can visualize a rose growing from the concrete. The rose symbolizes the person who is told they can't accomplish their dream. The visual imagery is used symbolically and means that you can achieve your dreams despite people's discouragement. The concrete is the dream that people say the "rose" can't accomplish, and "nature's law" is the people who say the "rose" can't do it.

EXERCISE 2

1. Describe the visual imagery you get when you read the poem *"I Know Why the Caged Bird Sings"* by Maya Angelou (1969).

> *The free bird leaps, on the back of the wind*
> *and floats downstream, till the current ends*
> *and dips his wings, in the orange sun rays*
> *and dares to claim the sky.*
> *But a bird that stalks, down his narrow cage*
> *can seldom see through, his bars of rage*
> *his wings are clipped and, his feet are tied*
> *so, he opens his throat to sing.*

_____

_____

2. What do you think the poem is about?

_____

_____

Literary Nonfiction

Literary nonfiction is a genre that uses literary devices to imitate a narrative. This means it often reads like a story, except the story is true, unlike fiction. The characters are real people, and the plot is based on real events. Some examples of works like this include diaries, journals, personal essays, biographies, autobiographies and memoirs.

Example

Humid air rolls through the cab, smelling of diesel and exhaust. The streets are mottled with evening shadows. From the back seat, I can feel the cab's engine idling when we stop. The tiny fists of street children crowd the open window beside me, clutching tight red buds already bending toward death. Brown eyes watch me from beneath tangled black hair. High-pitched voices seek something in a language I can't understand. The children are far too young to be wandering through traffic on darkening streets. I lean forward in my seat so the driver can hear me through the clouded plexiglass that separates us. "What are they saying?"

"They want to sell you the roses." I begin fumbling for my wallet.

"Ignore them," he says. His tone stops me, the reprimand clear.

The light changes and the cab lurches forward. The children barely have time to snatch their arms back. I want to save them all, but I may already be too late to claim even Luis.

An excerpt from *Becoming His Mother* by Mary A. Scherf (2015)

In the example above, you can experience the scene from the character's point of view. You can infer the character is traveling and is concerned about seeing children on the street. The text's descriptive language creates a clear image of the interaction between the character, the children and the cab driver.

When I was a teenager, I had two friends—Glick and Girson—who committed murder while robbing a mom-and-pop grocery store. This took place in Squirrel Hill, the well-to-do Pittsburgh neighborhood where I grew up, near the lovely, sprawling Frick Park and a short walk from the high school from which all three of us had recently graduated. The two old people who ran the store, Mr. and Mrs. Cua, were notoriously cranky, which made kids visit their store more often than necessary just to aggravate them, asking stupid questions or haggling over the price of a package of cigarettes or a can of Coke. The store was dirty and dusty, and the shelves were rather bare. No way could the Cuas have made enough to live on from that store—and in fact, there were constant and unsubstantiated rumors that they were hoarding mounds of cash in their living quarters in the back of the store. I never talked with anyone who knew where the rumors had started. It was just something we high school kids—freshmen to seniors—were always speculating about.

An excerpt from *True Crime* by Lee Gutkind (2013)

From the example above, you can experience the scene from the character's point of view. You can envision the scenes—the neighborhood as well as the store. The text's descriptive language creates a clear image of the place in which the character's friends committed murder.

PRACTICE EXERCISE

1. What can you infer from the following sentences? Discuss your answers with a classmate.

    a. The giant tree was ablaze with the orange, red and yellow leaves beginning to descend to the ground.

    _____

    _____

    b. The F-16 swooped down like an eagle after its prey.

    _____

    _____

2. Read the following lyrics from "Slow Dancing in a Burning Room" by John Mayer (2006).

    > It's not a silly little moment
    > It's not the storm before the calm
    > This is the deep and dyin' breath of
    > This love we've been workin' on
    > Can't seem to hold you like I want to
    > So I can feel you in my arms
    > Nobody's gonna come and save you
    > We pulled too many false alarms

    a. What comes to mind when you read the lyrics? Discuss your answer with a classmate.

    _____

    _____

    b. What imagery forms in your mind?

    _____

    _____

    _____

    c. What do you think is the theme of the lyrics?

    _____

    _____

    d. Can you make any text-to-self connections?

    _____

    _____

3. Read the following poem, *Preludes*, by T.S. Eliot (1911):

> *The winter evening settles down*
> *With smell of steaks in passageways.*
> *Six o'clock.*
> *The burnt-out ends of smoky days.*
> *And now a gusty shower wraps*
> *The grimy scraps*
> *Of withered leaves about your feet*
> *And newspapers from vacant lots;*
> *The showers beat*
> *On broken blinds and chimney-pots,*
> *And at the corner of the street*
> *A lonely cab-horse steams and stamps.*
> *And then the lighting of the lamps.*

a. What comes to mind when you read the poem? Discuss with a classmate.

_____

_____

b. What visual imagery comes to mind? Provide evidence.

_____

_____

_____

c. Can you detect auditory imagery as well? Provide evidence.

_____

_____

d. What is the poem's theme?

_____

4. Read the following personal essay excerpt from *Finding Sanctuary in Butterfly Town, USA* by Jennifer Lunden (2011).

> I grew up in a box-shaped house on a well-manicured lawn in the suburbs of a mid-sized Canadian city in Ontario. Across the road and abutting the river was a patch of city land, untended, wild, a field of tall grasses flecked with milkweed and Queen Anne's lace. There, I discovered my first monarch caterpillar. I was 9 years old, and I had never seen anything like it. Boldly ringed in concentric stripes—black, yellow and white—it was stretched out on a milkweed leaf, eating. I plucked it off, held it in my hand, touched it with my fingers. Its skin was smooth, leathery. It did not roll up in a ball. It did not seem afraid. Docile. I broke off the milkweed near the top and carried my find home.

a. What have you learned about the writer's childhood?

_____

_____

b. Can you make a text-to-self connection? Provide evidence.

_____

_____

c. In your own words, describe the imagery you get when reading the excerpt.

_____

_____

d. What is the person's reaction to discovering a monarch caterpillar? Provide evidence.

_____

_____

REFLECTION ON LEARNING

Answer the following reflection questions, and feel free to discuss your responses with your teacher or classmate.

- What reading idea or strategy did you learn from this section?

- What new concepts did you learn?

- What methods did you work on in this section?

- What aspect of this section is still not 100 percent clear for you?

- What do you want your teacher to know?

LESSON 11

ANALYZING NARRATIVE POINT OF VIEW

In every story, there is a narrator and a point of view. The author creates a narrator rather than telling the story himself. This narrator or storyteller describes the story's actions, characters and setting. The reader can learn a lot about this chronicler by reading his thoughts and feelings.

Recognizing the narrative point of view is an essential reading skill that helps you adopt the appropriate narration for your own writing. By the end of this lesson, you will learn to identify the types of narration: underline{first-person}, underline{third-person} and underline{first-third-person inversion}.

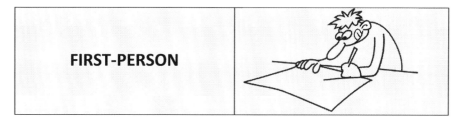

In first-person narration, the narrator tells the tale firsthand and usually doesn't know any other character's thoughts or feelings, so the reader doesn't either. First-person narration is easy to identify because the narrator will use first-person pronouns: *I, me, my, our, us, we, myself* and *ourselves*.

Examples

I woke up at 8 am, groggy and tired. I didn't sleep well and tossed and turned until my alarm went off. I was tempted to stay in bed, but I needed to get ready for work. If I were late again, my supervisor would have a fit. I threw my blankets aside and got up with my eyes half-closed.

From the example above, the writer uses the underlined terms to indicate the first-person narration. This passage is also told from the main character's point of view.

I ran to him at once, calling to my mother. But haste was all in vain. The captain had been struck dead by thundering apoplexy. It is a curious thing to understand, for I had certainly never liked the man, though of late I had begun to pity him, but as soon as I saw that he was dead, I burst into a flood of tears. It was the second death I had known, and the sorrow of the first was still fresh in my heart.

An excerpt from *Treasure Island* by Robert Louis Stevenson (1883)

From the example above, the writer uses the underlined words to indicate the first-person narration. You can understand how the captain's death impacted the main character as you get a direct account from him.

EXERCISE 1

The following excerpt is from *Black Beauty* by Anna Sewell (1877).

The first place that I can well remember was a large pleasant meadow with a pond of clear water in it. Some shady trees leaned over it, and rushes and water-lilies grew at the deep end. Over the hedge on one side we looked into a plowed field, and on the other we looked over a gate at our master's house, which stood by the roadside; at the top of the meadow was a grove of fir trees, and at the bottom a running brook overhung by a steep bank. While I was young I lived upon my mother's milk, as I could not eat grass. In the daytime I ran by her side, and at night I lay down close by her. When it was hot we used to stand by the pond in the shade of the trees, and when it was cold we had a nice warm shed near the grove. As soon as I was old enough to eat grass my mother used to go out to work in the daytime, and come back in the evening. There were six young colts in the meadow besides me; they were older than I was; some were nearly as large as grown-up horses. I used to run with them, and had great fun; we used to gallop all together round and round the field as hard as we could go. Sometimes we had rather rough play, for they would frequently bite and kick as well as gallop.

What evidence tells you this passage is written in the first-person narrative?

_____

| | THIRD-PERSON |

In third-person narrations, the narrator is not the main character, and third-person pronouns, such as *she, he* and *they*, are used. The words *I* and *me* are used only in dialogues. The reader may learn a little about the narrator but learns much more about the other characters.

Examples

Kelly took the car to the garage at around 2 pm this afternoon. She had noticed earlier in the week that the engine had a rattling noise every time she started or stopped the car. She was concerned that if the car wasn't looked at, it would give out, and she would be stuck on the highway. The car was due for maintenance anyway.

From the example above, the writer uses the underlined pronouns to indicate the third-person narration. You can understand that the character's fear her car may break down at any time has prompted her to take it to the garage for a check-up.

At half-past nine that night, Tom and Sid were sent to bed, as usual. They said their prayers, and Sid was soon asleep. Tom lay awake and waited in restless impatience. When it seemed to him that it must be nearly daylight, he heard the clock strike ten! This was despair. He would have tossed and fidgeted, as his nerves demanded, but he was afraid he might wake Sid. So he lay still and stared up into the dark. Everything was dismally still. By and by, out of the stillness, little, scarcely perceptible noises began to emphasize themselves. The ticking of the clock began to bring itself into notice.

An excerpt from *The Adventures of Tom Sawyer* by Mark Twain (1876)

From the example above, the writer uses the underlined words to indicate the third-person narration. We are provided with information about Tom and Sid, particularly the former character and his restless night.

EXERCISE 2

The following excerpt is from *A Tale of Two Cities* by Charles Dickens (1859).

Two other passengers, besides the one, were plodding up the hill by the side of the mail. All three were wrapped to the cheekbones and over the ears, and wore jack-boots. Not one of the three could have said, from anything he saw, what either of the other two was like; and each was hidden under almost as many wrappers from the eyes of the mind, as from the eyes of the body, of his two companions. In those days, travellers were very shy of being confidential on a short notice, for anybody on the road might be a robber or in league with robbers.

What evidence tells you this passage is written in the third-person narrative?

_____

_____

FIRST-THIRD-PERSON INVERSION

As a reader, you can rewrite first-person narratives into third-person narratives and vice-versa. This is particularly helpful when you are required to summarize a text in your own words.

Exercise 3

1. Using your own words, can you rewrite the following paragraph from first to third-person narration?

   To begin my life with the beginning of my life, I record that I was born (as I have been informed and believe) on a Friday, at twelve o'clock at night. It was remarked that the clock began to strike, and I began to cry, simultaneously.

   An excerpt from *David Copperfield* by Charles Dickens, 1850

_____

_____

2. Using your own words, can you rewrite the following statement from third to first-person narration?

   Since his papa's death, Cedric had found out that it was best not to talk to his mamma about him. When his father was ill, Cedric had been sent away, and when he had returned, everything was over...

   An excerpt from *Little Lord Fauntleroy* by Frances Hodgson Burnett, 1885

PRACTICE EXERCISE

1. Read the following passages. What type of narration is used: first or third-person?

a. Mr. Sherlock Holmes, who was usually very late in the mornings, save upon those not infrequent occasions when he was up all night, was seated at the breakfast table. I stood upon the hearth-rug and picked up the stick that our visitor had left behind him the night before. (An excerpt from *The Hound of the Baskervilles* by Sir Arthur Conan Doyle, 1902)	_____

b. At first I hated the school, but by and by I got so I could stand it. Whenever I got uncommon tired I played hookey, and the hiding I got next day done me good and cheered me up. So the longer I went to school the easier it got to be. (An excerpt from *The Adventures of Huckleberry Finn* by Mark Twain, 1884)	_____
c. Now, just after sundown, when all my work was over and I was on my way to my berth, it occurred to me that I should like an apple. I ran on deck. The watch was all forward looking out for the island. The man at the helm was watching the luff of the sail and whistling away gently to himself, and that was the only sound excepting the swish of the sea against the bows and around the sides of the ship. (An excerpt from *Treasure Island* by Robert Louis Stevenson, 1883)	_____
d. The clock struck six and, having swept up the hearth, Beth put a pair of slippers down to warm. Somehow the sight of the old shoes had a good effect upon the girls, for Mother was coming, and everyone brightened to welcome her. Meg stopped lecturing, and lighted the lamp, Amy got out of the easy chair without being asked, and Jo forgot how tired she was as she sat up to hold the slippers nearer to the blaze. (An excerpt from *Little Women*, 1868)	_____

2. Below is a passage from *The Call of the Wild* by Jack London (1903). It is a story about a dog, Buck, who is part St. Bernard and part collie. Rewrite the following passage from Buck's point of view.

> But Buck was neither house-dog nor kennel-dog. The whole realm was his. He plunged into the swimming tank or went hunting with the Judge's sons; he escorted Mollie and Alice, the Judge's daughters, on long twilight or early morning rambles; on wintry nights he lay at the Judge's feet before the roaring library fire; he carried the Judge's grandsons on his back, or rolled them in the grass, and guarded their footsteps through wild adventures down to the fountain in the stable yard, and even beyond, where the paddocks were, and the berry patches. Among the terriers he stalked imperiously, and Toots and Ysabel he utterly ignored, for he was king, —king over all creeping, crawling, flying things of Judge Miller's place, humans included.

_____

_____

_____

_____

_____

_____

_____

3. Read the excerpt below from *The Strange Case of Dr. Jekyll and Mr. Hyde* by Robert Louis Stevenson (1886). Rewrite the following passage from the woman's point of view.

> It was two o'clock when she came to herself and called for the police. The murderer was gone long ago; but there lay his victim in the middle of the lane, incredibly mangled. The stick with which the deed had been done, although it was of some rare and very tough and heavy wood, had broken in the middle under the stress of this insensate cruelty; and one splintered half had rolled in the neighboring gutter— the other, without doubt, had been carried away by the murderer. A purse and gold watch were found upon the victim: but no cards or papers, except a sealed and stamped envelope, which he had been probably carrying to the post, and which bore the name and address of Mr. Utterson.

_____

_____

_____

_____

_____

_____

_____

_____

_____

REFLECTION ON LEARNING

Answer the following reflection questions, and feel free to discuss your responses with your teacher or classmate.

- What reading idea or strategy did you learn from this section?

- What new concepts did you learn?

- What methods did you work on in this section?

- What aspect of this section is still not 100 percent clear for you?

- What do you want your teacher to know?

LESSON 12

LEARNING NONFICTION TEXT FEATURES

All forms of published material use graphic and organizational features to increase comprehension, organize content and add visual interest to the text. These are particularly present in nonfiction works. By the end of this lesson, you will learn what these features are and how they can help you locate information quickly and better understand your reading.

To illustrate, let us use snapshots of *The Principles of Psychology* by William James (1890), *The Frontier in American History* by Frederick Turner (1920) and *Personal Memoirs of U.S. Grant* by Ulysses S. Grant (1885).

TITLE The beginning of the page tells us the name of the book, the author, the publisher, place of publication, year of publication, etc. Name of the book: ***The Principles of Psychology,*** Author: ***William James*** Publisher: ***Henry Holt and Company*** Place of publication: ***New York*** 1. Can you answer the following questions based on the cover? a. What is the author's occupation? _____ b. What is the year of publication? _____ c. What volume is this book? _____	**THE PRINCIPLES** **OF** **PSYCHOLOGY** BY **WILLIAM JAMES** PROFESSOR OF PSYCHOLOGY IN HARVARD UNIVERSITY IN TWO VOLUMES VOL. I NEW YORK HENRY HOLT AND COMPANY 1918
PREFACE **This section gives a quick summary of what the book covers.** Can you answer the following question based on the excerpt? 2. Who is the intended audience of this book? _____	Excerpt from *The Principles of Psychology* by William James (1890) The treatise which follows has in the main grown up in connection with the author's class-room instruction in Psychology, although it is true that some of the chapters are more 'metaphysical,' and others fuller of detail, than is suitable for students who are going over the subject for the first time. The consequence of this is that, in spite of the exclusion of the important subjects of pleasure and pain, and moral and æsthetic feelings and judgments, the work has grown to a length which no one can regret more than the writer himself. The man must indeed be sanguine who, in this crowded age, can hope to have many readers for fourteen hundred continuous pages from his pen.

TABLE OF CONTENTS

This is the list of the topics in the book, and their corresponding page numbers.

3. a. How many chapters are there in *The Frontier In American History*?

_____

   b. Which chapter is the longest?

_____

Excerpt from *The Frontier in American History* by Frederick Turner (1920)

CONTENTS

INDEX

This is a list of important topics in the book with the page numbers in which they can be found.

4. Based on the image, which topic is covered extensively in *The Principles of Psychology*?

_____

Excerpt from *The Principles of Psychology* by William James (1890)

HEADING

This is the title of a page or section that tells the reader the topic they will be reading about.

5. What is the heading for Chapter VIII in *The Principles of Psychology*?

_____

Excerpt from *The Principles of Psychology* by William James (1890)

CHAPTER VII.

THE METHODS AND SNARES OF PSYCHOLOGY, 183

Psychology is a natural Science, 183. Introspection, 185. Experimen 'Psychologist's fallacy,' 196.

CHAPTER VIII.

THE RELATIONS OF MINDS TO OTHER THINGS, 199

Time relations: lapses of Consciousness—Locke v. Descartes, 200. The 'un 202. Minds may split into dissociated parts, 206. Space-relations: the Seat of The Psychologist's point of view, 218. Two kinds of knowledge, acquaintanc

SUBHEADING

In large books, subheadings are used to separate long sections into manageable chunks.

6. a. On what page does the subheading "The Psychologist's Point of View" start?

_____

    b. Under what heading does the subheading "Introspection" fall under?

_____

Excerpt from *The Principles of Psychology* by William James (1890)

CHAPTER VII.

THE METHODS AND SNARES OF PSYCHOLOGY, 183

Psychology is a natural Science, 183. Introspection, 185. Experimen 'Psychologist's fallacy,' 196.

CHAPTER VIII.

THE RELATIONS OF MINDS TO OTHER THINGS, 199

Time relations: lapses of Consciousness—Locke v. Descartes, 200. The 'un 202. Minds may split into dissociated parts, 206. Space-relations: the Seat of The Psychologist's point of view, 218. Two kinds of knowledge, acquaintanc

KEYWORDS

These are important words relating to a topic, and they usually stand out on the page. They may be in italics, bold, or highlighted in a different color from the rest of the text.

7. List at least FOUR keywords from the excerpt.

_____

Excerpt from *The Principles of Psychology* by William James (1890)

On the other hand, if we admit no *re-education* of centres, we not only fly in the face of an *a priori probability*, but we find ourselves compelled by facts to suppose an almost incredible number of functions natively lodged in the centres below the *thalami* or even in those below the *corpora quadrigemina*. I will consider the a priori objection after first taking a look at the facts which I have in mind. They confront us the moment we ask ourselves just *which are the parts which perform the functions abolished by an operation after sufficient time has elapsed for restoration to occur?*

ILLUSTRATIONS AND IMAGES

These visual cues are used to clarify the text. They can be captured using a scanner/camera or manually drawn.

8. Study the images from *The Principles of Psychology and Personal Memoirs Of U.S. Grant.* What do you think they depict?

_____

Excerpt from *The Principles of Psychology* by William James (1890)

This is an example of an illustration.

Excerpt from *Personal Memoirs of U.S. Grant* by Ulysses S. Grant (1885)

This is an example of a captured image.

CAPTIONS

This is a phrase, sentence or short paragraph that describes a picture. In non-fiction texts, images, diagrams and illustrations are all considered "figures."

9. What does the illustration from *The Principles of Psychology* show?

Excerpt from *The Principles of Psychology* by William James (1890)

FIG. 4.—The dotted lines stand for afferent paths, the broken lines for paths between the centres; the entire lines for efferent paths.

TABLES

These show a compressed analysis of the main points in a section. In scientific nonfiction books, tables may show the results of an experiment.

10. How many columns are there in the first excerpt? _____

11. According to the second excerpt, how many are missing from Raymond?

_____

12. In the first excerpt, where does "the desire to please and be noticed" fall under?

_____

13. In the second excerpt, which city has the highest number of wounded people?

Excerpt from *The Principles of Psychology* by William James (1890)

The empirical life of Self is divided, as below, into

	MATERIAL.	SOCIAL.	SPIRITUAL.
SELF-SEEKING.	Bodily Appetites and Instincts	Desire to please, be noticed, admired, etc.	Intellectual, Moral and Religious Aspiration, Conscientiousness.
	Love of Adornment, Foppery, Acquisitiveness, Constructiveness.	Sociability, Emulation, Envy, Love, Pursuit of Honor, Ambition, etc.	
	Love of Home, etc.		
SELF-ESTIMATION.	Personal Vanity, Modesty, etc.	Social and Family Pride, Vainglory, Snobbery, Humility, Shame, etc.	Sense of Moral or Mental Superiority, Purity, etc.
	Pride of Wealth, Fear of Poverty		Sense of Inferiority or of Guilt

Excerpt from *Personal Memoirs of U.S. Grant* by Ulysses S. Grant (1885)

	KILLED	WOUNDED	MISSING
Port Gibson	131	719	25
South Fork Bayou Pierre	..	1	..
Skirmishes, May 3	1	9	..
Fourteen Mile Creek	6	24	..
Raymond	66	339	39
Jackson	42	251	7
Champion's Hill	410	1,844	187
Big Black	39	237	3
Bridgeport	..	1	..
Total	695	3,425	259

CHARTS AND GRAPHS

These are drawings that explain information.

14. In one sentence, what can you infer from the excerpt?

_____

Excerpt from *The Principles of Psychology* **by William James (1890)**

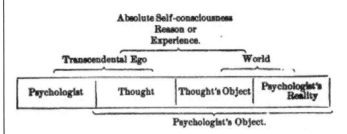

MAPS

These are representations that show the features of areas, such as lands, oceans or countries.

15. Can you name two states based on the excerpt?

_____

_____

16. In which state is Corinth?

_____

Excerpt from *Personal Memoirs of U.S. Grant* **by Ulysses S. Grant (1885)**

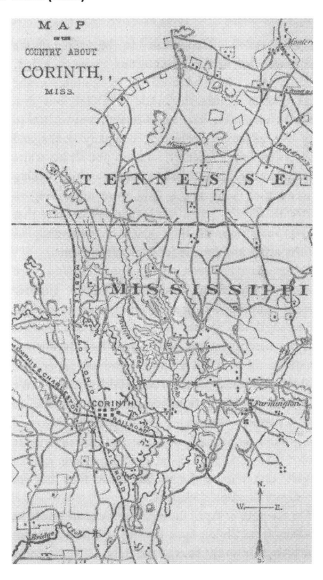

FOOTNOTES	Excerpt from *The Principles of Psychology* by William James (1890)
These are extra information used to support any statements made by the author or references that have been used in the text.	**FOOTNOTES:** [1:1] A paper read at the meeting of the American Historical Association in Chicago, July 12, 1893. It first appeared in the Proceedings of the State Historical Society of Wisconsin, December 14, 1893, with the following note: "The foundation of this paper is my article entitled 'Problems in American History,' which appeared in *The Ægis*, a publication of the students of the University of Wisconsin, November 4, 1892. . . . It is gratifying to find that Professor Woodrow Wilson—whose volume on 'Division and Reunion' in the Epochs of American History Series, has an appreciative estimate of the importance of the West as a factor in American history—accepts some of the views set forth in the papers above mentioned, and enhances their value by his lucid and suggestive treatment of them in his article in *The Forum*, December, 1893, reviewing Goldwin Smith's 'History of the United States.'" The present text is that of the *Report of the American Historical Association* for 1893, 199-227. It was printed with additions in the *Fifth Year Book of the National Herbart Society*, and in various other publications. [2:1] "Abridgment of Debates of Congress," v, p. 706. [5:1] Bancroft (1860 ed.), iii, pp. 344, 345, citing Logan MSS.; [Mitchell] "Contest in America," etc. (1752), p. 237. [5:2] Kercheval, "History of the Valley"; Bernheim, "German Settlements in the Carolinas"; Winsor, "Narrative and Critical History of America," v, p. 304; Colonial Records of North Carolina, iv, p. xx; Weston, "Documents Connected with the History of South Carolina," p. 82; Ellis and Evans, "History of Lancaster County, Pa.," chs. iii, xxvi. [5:3] Parkman, "Pontiac," ii; Griffis, "Sir William Johnson," p. 6; Simms's "Frontiersmen of New York." [5:4] Monette, "Mississippi Valley," i, p. 311

OTHER FEATURES

- Icons: These are small pictures that signal important information within the text.

- Timeline: This line shows the order in which events happened.

- Glossary: This is a list of the important words in a book, along with their meanings.

REFLECTION ON LEARNING

Answer the following reflection questions, and feel free to discuss your responses with your teacher or classmate.

- What reading idea or strategy did you learn from this section?

- What new concepts did you learn?

- What methods did you work on in this section?

- What aspect of this section is still not 100 percent clear for you?

- What do you want your teacher to know?

LESSON 13

FINAL THOUGHTS

You have reached the end of this manual. Congratulations! Each lesson focused on three main areas: vocabulary, reading comprehension skills and higher-order reading skills. Each used a variety of excerpts to make the connection between the focus areas. Do you remember that you filled out the first two sections of a K-W-L chart in the introduction section? Now is your chance to look back at it, and complete the last section.

WHAT HAVE I LEARNED?

A few final tips:

BEFORE READING

Why are you reading? Consider why you are reading and what you need to understand, know or do after reading. Keep this purpose in mind as you read.

Preview the text. Don't jump in all at once. Give the text an initial glance and consider reading introductions and conclusions to gather the main ideas.

Activate prior knowledge. Identify personal experiences or second-hand knowledge that relates to the topic. Make a list of things you want to know about the text or questions you want to try to answer while reading.

Break down your reading into manageable chunks. Taking breaks while reading improves focus, motivation, understanding and retention. Plus, it's healthier for our bodies!

WHILE READING

Monitor yourself. As soon as you notice your mind drifting, STOP and consider your needs. Before resuming, summarize the last chunk of text you remember to make sure that you understood and retained the information.

Annotate. Develop a system to note the following in the text: key ideas/major points, unfamiliar words/unclear information, keywords and phrases, relevant information and connections.

Summarize. After reading small sections of texts, identify the main ideas and two or three critical details in your own words. These summaries can serve as the basis for your notes while reading.

AFTER READING

What have you learned? Here, you can create an outline of the text from memory, discuss the material with a friend or ask yourself critical questions. These practices will help keep the information in your long-term memory for later use.

Read further. If any information remains unclear, locate other resources related to the topic, such as a trusted video source or web-based study guide.

Practice what you've learned. If you've learned a new phrase or word, use it in other forms of communication. This will help solidify the meaning in your mind, and you'll recall it easily the next time you come across it.

ASSESSMENT

READING PRACTICE TEST I

You will read multiple excerpts and answer 40 questions.
Your test time will be about 1 minute 44 seconds per question.
Your total time for this test is one hour (60 minutes).

Read and answer questions 1 to 8.

Fake News in the 1890s: Yellow Journalism
by Melissa Jacobs

Alternative facts, fake news, and post-truth have become common terms in the contemporary news industry. Today, social media platforms allow sensational news to "go viral," crowdsourced news from ordinary people to compete with professional reporting, and public figures in offices as high as the US presidency to bypass established media outlets when sharing news. However, dramatic reporting in daily news coverage predates the smartphone and tablet by over a century. In the late nineteenth century, the news media war between Joseph Pulitzer's *New York World* and William Randolph Hearst's *New York Journal* resulted in the rise of yellow journalism, as each newspaper used sensationalism and manipulated facts to increase sales and attract readers.

Many trace the origin of yellow journalism to coverage of the sinking of the USS Maine in Havana Harbor on February 15, 1898, and America's entry in the Spanish-American War. Both papers' reporting on this event featured sensational headlines, jaw-dropping images, bold fonts, and aggrandizement of facts, which influenced public opinion and helped incite America's involvement in what Hearst termed the "Journal's War."

The practice, and nomenclature, of yellow journalism actually predates the war, however. It originated with a popular comic strip character known as The Yellow Kid in Hogan's Alley. Created by Richard F. Outcault in 1895, Hogan's Alley was published in color by Pulitzer's *New York World*. When circulation increased at the *New York World*, William Randolph Hearst lured Outcault to his newspaper, the *New York Journal*. Pulitzer fought back by hiring another artist to continue the comic strip in his newspaper.

The period of peak yellow journalism by the two New York papers ended in the late 1890s, and each shifted priorities, but still included investigative exposés, partisan political coverage, and other articles designed to attract readers. Yellow journalism, past and present, conflicts with the principles of journalistic integrity. Today, media consumers will still encounter sensational journalism in print, on television, and online, as media outlets use eye-catching headlines to compete for audiences. To distinguish truth from "fake news," readers must seek multiple viewpoints, verify sources, and investigate evidence provided by journalists to support their claims.

1. **PART A**

   Which of the following options summarizes the main idea of the passage?

   a. Yellow journalism causes wars.

   b. Yellow journalism is a recent phenomenon.

   c. Yellow journalism is used to attract readers and increase sales.

   d. Yellow journalism accurately depicts world events.

PART B

Which of the following sentences from the passage supports your answer to PART A?

a. Today, media consumers still encounter sensational journalism in print, on television, and online, as media outlets use eye-catching headlines to compete for audiences.

b. Pulitzer fought back by hiring another artist to continue the comic strip in his newspaper.

c. However, dramatic reporting in daily news coverage predates the smartphone and tablet by over a century.

d. The practice, and nomenclature, of yellow journalism actually predates the war, however.

COACHING FOR BETTER LEARNING

2. What is the meaning of the word **aggrandizement** as used in this sentence from the passage?

> Both papers' reporting on this event featured sensational headlines, jaw-dropping images, bold fonts, and **aggrandizement** of facts, which influenced public opinion and helped incite America's involvement in what Hearst termed the "Journal's War."

   a. Eloquent
   b. Forthcoming
   c. Summarizing
   d. Exaggeration

3. What is the earliest account of Yellow Journalism?

   a. Coverage of the presidential campaign in 1895
   b. Coverage of the sinking of the USS Maine in Havana Harbor in 1898
   c. A popular comic strip known as Hogan's Valley
   d. When *New York World* hired Richard F. Outcault

4. **PART A**

   What does the writer recommend to do to distinguish between true news and sensationalist news?

   a. Investigate evidence.
   b. Believe one journalistic point of view.
   c. Disprove all journalism.
   d. None of the above.

   PART B

   Which of the following sentences from the passage supports your answer to PART A?

   a. The period of peak yellow journalism by the two New York papers ended in the late 1890s, and each shifted priorities. However, both still included investigative exposés, partisan political coverage, and other articles designed to attract readers.
   b. However, dramatic reporting in daily news coverage predates the smartphone and tablet by over a century.
   c. To distinguish truth from "fake news," readers must seek multiple viewpoints, verify sources, and investigate evidence provided by journalists to support their claims.
   d. Yellow journalism, past and present, conflicts with the principles of journalistic integrity.

5. Which of the following terms IS NOT commonly used to refer to the news?

   a. Alternative facts
   b. Fake news
   c. Post-truth
   d. Absolute truth

6. When did America enter the Spanish-American war?

   a. 1998
   b. 1898
   c. 1988
   d. 1888

7. **PART A**
To increase readership, what did William Randolph Hearst do?

   a. Sold his newspaper agency
   b. Retired
   c. Hired Richard F. Outcault
   d. Fired Richard F. Outcault

PART B.
What did Joseph Pulitzer do in retaliation?

   a. Hired Richard F. Outcault
   b. Hired another artist
   c. Hired William Randolph Hearst
   d. Bought William Randolph Hearst's newspaper agency

8. What is the name of the character in Hogan's Alley?

   a. The Blue Kid
   b. The Yellow Kid
   c. The Sensitive Kid
   d. The Wild Kid

Read the poem below by Charles Bukowski and answer questions 9 to 12.

ALONE WITH EVERYBODY

the flesh covers the bone,
and they put a mind,
in there and,
sometimes a soul,
and the women break,
vases against the walls
and the men drink too,
much
and nobody finds the,
one but keep looking,
crawling in and out, of beds.
flesh covers, the bone and the
flesh searches, for more than
flesh.

there's no chance,
at all:
we are all trapped, by a singular
fate.
nobody ever finds, the one.

the city dumps fill, the junkyards fill
the madhouses fill, the hospitals fill
the graveyards fill

nothing else, fills.

9. **PART A**
Which of the following describes the main idea in the poem?

   a. We can feel alone even in a crowd of people.
   b. Flesh covers the bone.
   c. Men are alcoholics.
   d. Women destroy property.

PART B
Which of the following sentences supports your answer in PART A?

   a. the city dumps fill, the junkyards fill
   b. the flesh covers the bone
   c. flesh searches, for more than/ flesh.
   d. and the women break,/ vases against the walls

10. Which sense/s does the poet draw on?
    a. Sight
    b. Sight and smell
    c. Sight and hearing
    d. Hearing

11. **PART A**

   Read the following excerpt from the poem:

   the city dumps fill, the junkyards fill
   the madhouses fill, the hospitals fill
   the graveyards fill
   nothing else, fills.

   What emotion can you infer from it?
    a. Joy
    b. Hopelessness
    c. Anger
    d. Contentment

   PART B

   What literary device has been used?

    a. Hyperbole

    b. Simile

    c. Repetition

    d. Alliteration

12. Break down the following words and write the root word and prefix/suffix.

Word	Prefix	Root word	Suffix
Telephone			
Description			
Artist			
Disrespect			

Read this excerpt from a poem titled "Knitting the Socks," and answer questions 13 to 16.

By the fireside, cozily seated,
With spectacles riding her nose,
The lively old lady is knitting
A wonderful pair of hose.
She pities the shivering soldier,
Who is out in the pelting storm,
And busily plies her needles
To keep him hearty and warm.

Her eyes are reading the embars,
But her heart is off to the war,
For she knows what those brave fellows,
Are gallantly fighting for.
She ponders how in her childhood,
Her grandmother used to tell
The story of barefoot soldiers,
Who fought for so long and well.

And the men of the Revolution,
Are nearer to her than us;
And that perhaps is the reason
Why she is toiling thus.
She cannot shoulder a musket,
Nor ride with the cavalry crew,
But nevertheless she is ready
To work for the boys who do

So prithee, proud owner of muscle,
Or purse proud owner of stocks,
Don't sneer at the labors of woman
Or smile at her bundle of socks.
Her heart may be larger and braver
Than his who is tallest of all,
And the work of her hands as important
As cash that buys powder and ball.

13. How many stanzas does the excerpt have?

    a. 4

    b. 2

    c. 3

    d. 5

14. What is the poem about?

    a. Women hand-knitting socks for Civil War soldiers

    b. Women sitting at home praying for Civil War soldiers

    c. Women putting in as much effort in the war as men

    d. Never judging a book by its cover

15. In the third stanza, who is ready to work for the soldiers?

    a. No one

    b. The poet

    c. The old lady

    d. The soldiers themselves

16. **PART A**

What is the main idea of the last four lines of the final stanza?

    a. The old lady deserves respect for her input in the war.

    b. The old lady is tired of knitting socks.

    c. The speaker doesn't like the patterns on the socks.

    d. The speaker has decided to enlist.

PART B

What literary device has been used in that section?

    a. Hyperbole

    b. Alliteration

    c. Simile

    d. Rhyming

The following is an advertisement published in The American Anti-Slavery Almanac, 1838. Read through the ad and answer questions 16 to 20.

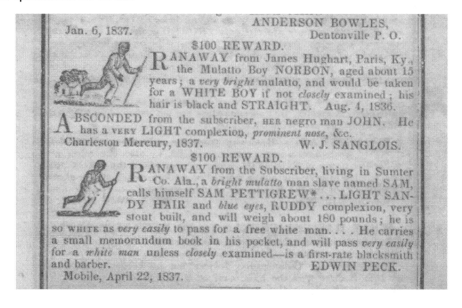

17. **PART A**

Using a text-to-world connection, what is the main topic of the advertisement?

a. Racism

b. Slavery

c. Price reductions

d. Running away from home

PART B

Which of the following summarizes the main idea in the advertisement?

a. Readers are asked to look out for a few runaway slaves.

b. There will be an auctioning of slaves at the city's square.

c. Readers are informed of a reduction in prices for new homes.

d. The government is announcing the availability of funding for personal projects.

18. Who carries a book as a small memorandum?

a. Norbon

b. Edwin Peck

c. Sam Pettigrew

d. John

19. What does the term *mulatto* mean?

a. It is an offensive term that refers to a person of mixed racial descent.

b. It is an offensive term that refers to a person's weight.

c. It is an offensive term that refers to a person's height.

d. It is an offensive term that refers to a person's personality.

20. Which of the following words is closest in meaning to *abscond*?

a. Jogging

b. Escape

c. Dance

d. Retaliate

Answer questions 21 to 23 that are based on the following lyrics from "Titanium" by David Guetta featuring Sia.

> *You shout it out*
> *But I can't hear a word you say*
> *I'm talking loud not saying much*
> *I'm criticized but all your bullets ricochet*
> *You shoot me down, but I get up*
> *I'm bulletproof nothing to lose*
> *Fire away, fire away*
> *Ricochet, you take your aim*
> *Fire away, fire away*
> *You shoot me down but I won't fall, I am titanium*
> *You shoot me down but I won't fall*
> *I am titanium, I am titanium, I am titanium, I am titanium*

21. What is the main idea of this song?

    a. Others' opinions should not deter one from fulfilling one's desires.
    b. Others' opinions should impact one's decisions.
    c. You should remain strong and healthy.
    d. Others' opinions are invalid, but you should still give up.

22. Which literary device is used?
    a. Synonym
    b. Metaphor
    c. Alliteration
    d. Simile

23. In this context, what does "titanium" mean?
    a. Weak-willed
    b. Strong-willed
    c. Elated
    d. Purgatory

Read the following excerpt from *Peter Pan* by James M. Barrie (1902), then answer questions 24 to 30.

Hook was fighting now without hope. That passionate breast no longer asked for life; but for one boon it craved: to see Peter show bad form before it was cold forever.

Abandoning the fight he rushed into the powder magazine and fired it.

"In two minutes," he cried, "the ship will be blown to pieces."

Now, now, he thought, true form will show.

But Peter issued from the powder magazine with the shell in his hands, and calmly flung it overboard.

What sort of form was Hook himself showing? Misguided man though he was, we may be glad, without sympathising with him, that in the end he was true to the traditions of his race. The other boys were flying around him now, flouting, scornful; and he staggered about the deck striking up at them impotently, his mind was no longer with them; it was slouching in the playing fields of long ago, or being sent up [to the headmaster] for good, or watching the wall-game from a famous wall. And his shoes were right, and his waistcoat was right, and his tie was right, and his socks were right.

James Hook, thou not wholly unheroic figure, farewell.

For we have come to his last moment.

Seeing Peter slowly advancing upon him through the air with dagger poised, he sprang upon the bulwarks to cast himself into the sea. He did not know that the crocodile was waiting for him; for we purposely stopped the clock that this knowledge might be spared him: a little mark of respect from us at the end.

He had one last triumph, which I think we need not grudge him. As he stood on the bulwark looking over his shoulder at Peter gliding through the air, he invited him with a gesture to use his foot. It made Peter kick instead of stab.

At last Hook had got the boon for which he craved.

"Bad form," he cried jeeringly, and went content to the crocodile.

Thus perished James Hook.

"Seventeen," Slightly sang out; but he was not quite correct in his figures. Fifteen paid the penalty for their crimes that night; but two reached the shore: Starkey to be captured by the redskins, who made him nurse for all their papooses, a melancholy come-down for a pirate; and Smee, who henceforth wandered about the world in his spectacles, making a precarious living by saying he was the only man that Jas. Hook had feared.

Wendy, of course, had stood by taking no part in the fight, though watching Peter with glistening eyes; but now that all was over she became prominent again. She praised them equally, and shuddered delightfully when Michael showed her the place where he had killed one; and then she took them into Hook's cabin and pointed to his watch which was hanging on a nail. It said "half-past one!"

The lateness of the hour was almost the biggest thing of all. She got them to bed in the pirates' bunks pretty quickly, you may be sure; all but Peter, who strutted up and down on the deck, until at last he fell asleep by the side of Long Tom. He had one of his dreams that night, and cried in his sleep for a long time, and Wendy held him tightly.

24. **PART A**

What is the main idea in the excerpt?

a. James Hook was killed by Peter Pan.

b. Peter Pan killed Wendy.

c. Wendy killed James Hook.

d. James Hook was killed by a crocodile.

PART B

Which of the following sentences support your answer in PART A?

a. The lateness of the hour was almost the biggest thing of all.

b. Thus perished James Hook.

c. But Peter issued from the powder magazine with the shell in his hands, and calmly flung it overboard.

d. "Bad form," he cried jeeringly, and went content to the crocodile.

25. How many people should have paid their penalties that night?

a. 12

b. 17

c. 15

d. 10

26. **PART A**

What does the writer mean in this line?

"...and he staggered about the deck striking up at them *impotently*, his mind was no longer with them..."

a. Peter Pan was helpless to the onslaught.

b. James Hook was helpless to the onslaught.

c. Wendy was helpless to the onslaught.

d. James Hook was hopeful he could win.

PART B

Which of the following options is an appropriate alternative to the word in bold?

a. Powerful

b. Helpful

c. Helpless

d. Hopeful

27. Where did Peter fall asleep?
    a. In the pirates' bunks
    b. On the beach
    c. Beside Wendy
    d. By the side of Long Tom

28. What did the redskins make Starkey do?
    a. Marry their sister.
    b. Nurse their papooses.
    c. Nurse their children.
    d. Kill their enemies.

29. Choose the option which best corrects the errors in this sentence.

    Passed experience tells me sitting in a draft you'll catch a cold.

    a. Passed experience tells me if I sat in a draught, you'll catch a cold.
    b. Past experience tells me if I sit in a draft, I'll catch a cold.
    c. Passed experience tells me if I catch a cold, I should sit in a draught.
    d. Past experience tells me if I sit in a draught, I'll catch a cold.

30. Which of the following words is a suitable alternative to the underlined word?

    A tour leader needs to be a sociable person.

    a. Grateful

    b. Angry

    c. Gregarious

    d. Impetuous

Read the following passage from *Alice's Adventures in Wonderland* by Lewis Carroll (1865) to answer questions 31 to 35.

So she swallowed one of the cakes, and was delighted to find that she began shrinking directly. As soon as she was small enough to get through the door, she ran out of the house, and found quite a crowd of little animals and birds waiting outside. The poor little Lizard, Bill, was in the middle, being held up by two guinea-pigs, who were giving it something out of a bottle. They all made a rush at Alice the moment she appeared; but she ran off as hard as she could, and soon found herself safe in a thick wood.

"The first thing I've got to do," said Alice to herself, as she wandered about in the wood, "is to grow to my right size again; and the second thing is to find my way into that lovely garden. I think that will be the best plan."

It sounded an excellent plan, no doubt, and very neatly and simply arranged; the only difficulty was, that she had not the smallest idea how to set about it; and while she was peering about anxiously among the trees, a little sharp bark just over her head made her look up in a great hurry.

An enormous puppy was looking down at her with large round eyes, and feebly stretching out one paw, trying to touch her. "Poor little thing!" said Alice, in a coaxing tone, and she tried hard to whistle to it; but she was terribly frightened all the time at the thought that it might be hungry, in which case it would be very likely to eat her up in spite of all her coaxing.

Hardly knowing what she did, she picked up a little bit of stick, and held it out to the puppy; whereupon the puppy jumped into the air off all its feet at once, with a yelp of delight, and rushed at the stick, and made believe to worry it; then Alice dodged behind a great thistle, to keep herself from being run over; and the moment she appeared on the other side, the puppy made another rush at the stick, and tumbled head over heels in its hurry to get hold of it; then Alice, thinking it was very like having a game of play with a cart-horse, and expecting every moment to be trampled under its feet, ran round the thistle again; then the puppy began a series of short charges at the stick, running a very little way forwards each time and a long way back, and barking hoarsely all the while, till at last it sat down a good way off, panting, with its tongue hanging out of its mouth, and its great eyes half shut.

This seemed to Alice a good opportunity for making her escape; so she set off at once, and ran till she was quite tired and out of breath, and till the puppy's bark sounded quite faint in the distance.

31. **PART A**

What is the main idea in this passage?

a. Alice is sad that she can't play with her friends.

b. Alice doesn't know how to grow back into her normal size and runs into a problem.

c. Alice is a giant, unaware of the distraction she is causing.

d. Alice runs into a puppy that she likes.

PART B

Which of the following sentences supports your answer in PART A?

a. This seemed to Alice a good opportunity for making her escape; so she set off at once, and ran till she was quite tired and out of breath, and till the puppy's bark sounded quite faint in the distance.

b. The only difficulty was that she had not the smallest idea how to set about it;

c. Hardly knowing what she did, she picked up a little bit of stick, and held it out to the puppy;

d. As soon as she was small enough to get through the door, she ran out of the house and found quite a crowd of little animals and birds waiting outside.

32. **PART A**

What is Alice afraid of in this passage?

a. The puppy
b. Herself
c. The universe
d. Her mother

PART B

What does she do to solve this problem?

a. She cries.
b. She sits down and talks to herself.
c. She plays with the puppy.
d. She gives the puppy a stick to play with, and it runs off.

33. How many characters are in this story?

a. 1
b. 4
c. 5
d. 2

34. What emotion did the puppy display when it saw the stick?

a. Sadness
b. Happiness
c. Anger
d. Irritation

35. **PART A**

What did the writer mean in this line?

*"...then Alice, thinking it was very like having a game of play with a cart-horse, and expecting every moment to be **trampled** under its feet, ran round the thistle again..."*

a. Alice was afraid that the dog would kill her.
b. Alice was exercising with her newfound pet.
c. Alice was having a lot of fun playing with the puppy.

d. Alice was sad because the puppy did not want to play with her.

PART B

Which of the following is a suitable alternative for the underlined word?
a. Crushed
b. Molded
c. Triumphed
d. Built

Read the following excerpt from *Personal Memoirs of U.S. Grant* by Ulysses S. Grant (1885) and answer questions 36 to 40.

The route followed by the army from Puebla to the City of Mexico was over Rio Frio mountain, the road leading over which, at the highest point, is about eleven thousand feet above tide water. The pass through this mountain might have been easily defended, but it was not; and the advanced division reached the summit in three days after leaving Puebla. The City of Mexico lies west of Rio Frio mountain, on a plain backed by another mountain six miles farther west, with others still nearer on the north and south. Between the western base of Rio Frio and the City of Mexico there are three lakes, Chalco and Xochimilco on the left and Texcoco on the right, extending to the east end of the City of Mexico. Chalco and Texcoco are divided by a narrow strip of land over which the direct road to the city runs. Xochimilco is also to the left of the road, but at a considerable distance south of it, and is connected with Lake Chalco by a narrow channel. There is a high rocky mound, called El Penon, on the right of the road, springing up from the low flat ground dividing the lakes. This mound was strengthened by intrenchments at its base and summit, and rendered a direct attack impracticable.

Scott's army was rapidly concentrated about Ayotla and other points near the eastern end of Lake Chalco. Reconnoissances were made up to within gun-shot of El Penon, while engineers were seeking a route by the south side of Lake Chalco to flank the city, and come upon it from the south and south-west. A way was found around the lake, and by the 18th of August troops were in St. Augustin Tlalpam, a town about eleven miles due south from the plaza of the capital. Between St. Augustin Tlalpam and the city lie the hacienda of San Antonio and the village of Churubusco, and south-west of them is Contreras. All these points, except St. Augustin Tlalpam, were intrenched and strongly garrisoned. Contreras is situated on the side of a mountain, near its base, where volcanic rocks are piled in great confusion, reaching nearly to San Antonio. This made the approach to the city from the south very difficult.

The brigade to which I was attached—Garland's, of Worth's division—was sent to confront San Antonio, two or three miles from St. Augustin Tlalpam, on the road to Churubusco and the City of Mexico. The ground on which San Antonio stands is completely in the valley, and the surface of the land is only a little above the level of the lakes, and, except to the south-west, it was cut up by deep ditches filled with water. To the south-west is the Pedregal—the volcanic rock before spoken of—over which cavalry or artillery could not be passed, and infantry would make but poor progress if confronted by an enemy. From the position occupied by Garland's brigade, therefore, no movement could be made against the defences of San Antonio except to the front, and by a narrow causeway, over perfectly level ground, every inch of which was commanded by the enemy's artillery and infantry. If Contreras, some three miles west and south, should fall into our hands, troops from there could move to the right flank of all the positions held by the enemy between us and the city. Under these circumstances General Scott directed the holding of the front of the enemy without making an attack until further orders.

On the 18th of August, the day of reaching San Augustin Tlalpam, Garland's brigade secured a position within easy range of the advanced intrenchments of San Antonio, but where his troops were protected by an artificial embankment that had been thrown up for some other purpose than defense.

36. Which of the following is NOT a lake found between the western base of Rio Frio and the City of Mexico?

    a. Chalco
    b. Texcoco
    c. Texmilco
    d. Xochmilco

37. Which POV is the narration of the excerpt primarily in?

    a. First-person
    b. Second-person
    c. Third-person
    d. Fourth-person

38. **PART A**

What does the writer mean in this sentence?

*Scott's army was rapidly **concentrated** about Ayotla and other points near the eastern end of Lake Chalco.*

    a. Scott's army was located in different countries.
    b. Scott's army was located in different locations in Mexico.
    c. Scott's army was located in different locations surrounding San Antonia.
    d. Scott's army was located only in Lake Chalco.

PART B

Which of the following is a suitable antonym for the underlined word?
    a. Present
    b. Absent
    c. Dead
    d. Alive

39. When did Garland's brigade reach San Augustin Tlalpam?
    a. 18th of August
    b. 12th of August
    c. 18th of May
    d. 19th of August

40. Which mound divided the three lakes?
    a. Mt Kilimanjaro
    b. El Penon
    c. El Mexica
    d. El Chalco

ASSESSMENT

READING PRACTICE TEST II

You will read multiple passages and answer 40 questions.
Your test time will be about 1 minute 44 seconds per question.
Your total time for this test is one hour (60 minutes).

Read the following excerpt from *The Adventures of Tom Sawyer* by Mark Twain (1876) and answer questions 1 to 8.

About midnight Tom arrived with a boiled ham and a few trifles, and stopped in a dense undergrowth on a small bluff overlooking the meeting-place. It was starlight, and very still. The mighty river lay like an ocean at rest. Tom listened a moment, but no sound disturbed the quiet. Then he gave a low, distinct whistle. It was answered from under the bluff. Tom whistled twice more; these signals were answered in the same way. Then a guarded voice said:

"Who goes there?"

"Tom Sawyer, the Black Avenger of the Spanish Main. Name your names."

"Huck Finn the Red-Handed, and Joe Harper the Terror of the Seas." Tom had furnished these titles from his favorite literature.

"'Tis well. Give the countersign."

Two hoarse whispers delivered the same awful word simultaneously to the brooding night:

"Blood!"

Then Tom tumbled his ham over the bluff and let himself down after it, tearing both skin and clothes to some extent in the effort. There was an easy, comfortable path along the shore under the bluff, but it lacked the advantages of difficulty and danger so valued by a pirate.

The Terror of the Seas had brought a side of bacon, and had about worn himself out with getting it there. Finn the Red-Handed had stolen a skillet and a quantity of half-cured leaf tobacco, and had also brought a few corn-cobs to make pipes with. But none of the pirates smoked or "chewed" but himself. The Black Avenger of the Spanish Main said it would never do to start without some fire. That was a wise thought; matches were hardly known there in that day. They saw a fire smouldering upon a great raft a hundred yards above, and they went stealthily thither and helped themselves to a chunk. They made an imposing adventure of it, saying, "Hist!" every now and then, and suddenly halting with finger on lip; moving with hands on imaginary dagger-hilts; and giving orders in dismal whispers that if "the foe" stirred, to "let him have it to the hilt," because "dead men tell no tales." They knew well enough that the raftsmen were all down at the village laying in stores or having a spree, but still that was no excuse for their conducting this thing in an unpiratical way.

1. **PART A**

Which of the following is the main idea of the passage?

    a. Tom, Huck and Joe meet to consume their stolen goods together.

    b. Tom, Huck and Joe are captured by the raftsmen for stealing.

    c. Tom, Huck and Joe do not like each other.

    d. Tom, Huck and Joe are reliving their time as raftsmen.

PART B

Which of the following sentences from the passage supports your answer to PART A?

    a. Finn the Red-Handed had stolen a skillet and a quantity of half-cured leaf tobacco, and had also brought a few corn-cobs to make pipes with.

    b. They knew well enough that the raftsmen were all down at the village laying in stores or having a spree, but still that was no excuse for their conducting this thing in an unpiratical way.

    c. Two hoarse whispers delivered the same awful word simultaneously to the brooding night.

    d. "Who goes there?"

2. **PART A**

Which of the following is NOT a nickname assigned to the boys?

a. Finn the Red-Handed
b. Tom Sawyer, the Black Avenger of the Spanish Main
c. Joe Harper, the Terror of the Seas
d. Tom Sawyer, the Red Avenger of the Spanish Main

PART B

Who furnished these nicknames?

a. Finn the Red-Handed
b. Tom Sawyer, the Red Avenger of the Spanish Main
c. Tom Sawyer, the Black Avenger of the Spanish Main
d. Joe Harper, the Terror of the Seas

3. What type of literary device is used in the phrase, *"dead men tell no tales"*?
    a. Simile
    b. Proverb
    c. Hyperbole
    d. Alliteration

4. **PART A**

What type of narration is being used in this paragraph?

> They made an imposing adventure of it, saying, "Hist!" every now and then, and suddenly halting with finger on lip; moving with hands on imaginary dagger-hilts; and giving orders in dismal whispers that if "the foe" stirred, to "let him have it to the hilt," because "dead men tell no tales." They knew well enough that the raftsmen were all down at the village laying in stores or having a spree, but still that was no excuse for their conducting this thing in an unpiratical way.

    a. Second
    b. Third
    c. First
    d. Tom's

PART B

Which of the following options summarizes what is happening in this excerpt?
    a. The boys are exaggerating their actions.
    b. The boys are scared of waking up any of the raftsmen.
    c. The boys have dagger-hilts attached to their hips.
    d. The raftsmen are their friends.

5. Are Huck and Joe together when Tom approaches their meeting place?
    a. Huck is alone.
    b. Joe is alone.
    c. They are together.
    d. Tom doesn't find anyone at the meeting place.

6. **PART A**

At what time of day is this scene taking place?
    a. At noon
    b. At 8 am
    c. At 8 pm
    d. At midnight

PART B

Which of the following statements supports your answer to PART A?

a. The Terror of the Seas had brought a side of bacon, and had about worn himself out with getting it there.

b. "Tom Sawyer, the Black Avenger of the Spanish Main. Name your names."

c. About midnight Tom arrived with a boiled ham and a few trifles, and stopped in a dense undergrowth on a small bluff overlooking the meeting-place.

d. Then he gave a low, distinct whistle.

7. **PART A**

What type of text construction is used in the paragraph below?

Although I raised Mercy and Calum from young kittens, they have different temperaments. Calum is seven years old and Persian breed, whereas Mercy is the same age, but a Maine Coon. Calum insists on sleeping on the bed, but Mercy is okay with sleeping on the floor. They may be the same age, but Calum seems uptight and protective. On the other hand, Mercy is hyper and friendly. Given that they were both treated the same way all their life, it is hard to believe that they are so different in everything they do.

a. Cause-and-effect

b. Compare-and-contrast

c. Figurative language

d. None of the above

PART B

Which of the following statements DOES NOT describe the writer?

a. They are observant.

b. They are knowledgeable about cat breeds.

c. They like Mercy more than Calum.

d. They like their cats equally.

8. Read each sentence below. If the sentence contains a hyperbole, write "hyperbole" in the blank. If it does not have one, write "none" in the blank.

a. As I approached the horse, it seemed larger than it had in the pasture. _____

b. The dog was so dirty that it had a tomato plant growing on its back. _____

c. Larry acted like such a big baby that his parents had to use bed sheets for diapers. _____

Read the following excerpt from *Common Sense* by Thomas Paine (1776) and answer questions 9 to 14.

Volumes have been written on the subject of the struggle between England and America. Men of all ranks have embarked in the controversy, from different motives, and with various designs; but all have been ineffectual, and the period of debate is closed. Arms, as the last resource, decide the contest; the appeal was the choice of the king, and the continent hath accepted the challenge.

It hath been reported of the late Mr. Pelham (who tho' an able minister was not without his faults) that on his being attacked in the house of commons, on the score, that his measures were only of a temporary kind, replied *"they will last my time."* Should a thought so fatal and unmanly possess the colonies in the present contest, the name of ancestors will be remembered by future generations with detestation.

The sun never shined on a cause of greater worth. 'Tis not the affair of a city, a country, a province, or a kingdom, but of a continent—of at least one eighth part of the habitable globe. 'Tis not the concern of a day, a year, or an age; posterity are virtually involved in the contest, and will be more or less affected, even to the end of time, by the proceedings now. Now is the seed time of continental union, faith and honor. The least fracture now will be like a name engraved with the point of a pin on the tender rind of a young oak; the wound will enlarge with the tree, and posterity read it in full grown characters.

By referring the matter from argument to arms, a new era for politics is struck; a new method of thinking hath arisen. All plans, proposals, &c. prior to the nineteenth of April, *i.e.* to the commencement of hostilities, are like the almanacks of the last year; which, though proper then, are superseded and useless now. Whatever was advanced by the advocates on either side of the question then, terminated in one and the same point, viz. a union with Great-Britain; the only difference between the parties was the method of effecting it; the one proposing force, the other friendship; but it hath so far happened that the first hath failed, and the second hath withdrawn her influence.

As much hath been said of the advantages of reconciliation, which, like an agreeable dream, hath passed away and left us as we were, it is but right, that we should examine the contrary side of the argument, and inquire into some of the many material injuries which these colonies sustain, and always will sustain, by being connected with, and dependent on Great-Britain. To examine that connexion and dependence, on the principles of nature and common sense, to see what we have to trust to, if separated, and what we are to expect, if dependent.

I have heard it asserted by some, that as America hath flourished under her former connexion with Great-Britain, that the same connexion is necessary towards her future happiness, and will always have the same effect. Nothing can be more fallacious than this kind of argument. We may as well assert that because a child has thrived upon milk, that it is never to have meat, or that the first twenty years of our lives is to become a precedent for the next twenty. But even this is admitting more than is true, for I answer roundly, that America would have flourished as much, and probably much more, had no European power had any thing to do with her.

The commerce, by which she hath enriched herself are the necessaries of life, and will always have a market while eating is the custom of Europe.

But she has protected us, say some. That she has engrossed us is true, and defended the continent at our expense as well as her own is admitted, and she would have defended Turkey from the same motive, viz. the sake of trade and dominion.

9. **PART A**

What is the main idea in this extract?

a. Mr. Pelham's strategy is a long-term solution.

b. America is dependent on England to provide food.

c. Reconciliation never works.

d. America would have still thrived even without striking a deal with England.

PART B

Which of the following sentences from the passage supports your answer in PART A?

a. By referring the matter from argument to arms, a new era for politics is struck; a new method of thinking hath arisen.

b. But even this is admitting more than is true, for I answer roundly, that America would have flourished as much, and probably much more, had no European power had anything to do with her.

c. I have heard it asserted by some, that as America hath flourished under her former connexion with Great-Britain, that the same connexion is necessary towards her future happiness, and will always have the same effect.

d. The commerce, by which she hath enriched herself are the necessaries of life, and will always have a market while eating is the custom of Europe.

10. **PART A**

What last resource decided whether countries would go to war?

a. Pride

b. Arms

c. Lack of food

d. Mr. Pelham

PART B

Which of the following sentences from the passage supports your answer to PART A?

a. It hath been reported of the late Mr. Pelham (who tho' an able minister was not without his faults) that on his being attacked in the house of commons, on the score, that his measures were only of a temporary kind, replied *"they will last my time."*

b. All plans, proposals, &c. prior to the nineteenth of April, *i.e.* to the commencement of hostilities, are like the almanacks of the last year; which, though proper then, are superseded and useless now.

c. Arms, as the last resource, decide the contest; the appeal was the choice of the king, and the continent hath accepted the challenge.

d. But she has protected us, say some.

11. Read the following sentence from the passage:

   Should a thought so fatal and unmanly possess the colonies in the present contest, the name of ancestors will be remembered by future generations with <u>detestation</u>.

   Which of the following options is an alternative to the underlined word?

a. Intense love

b. Intense indifference

c. Intense taste

d. Intense dislike

12. To whom is the writer referring in this sentence?

But she has protected us, say some.

a. America
b. China

c. England
d. Germany

13. **PART A**

What does the writer mean in this statement?

I have heard it asserted by some, that as America hath flourished under her former connexion with Great-Britain, that the same connexion is necessary towards her future happiness, and will always have the same effect. Nothing can be more fallacious than this kind of argument.

a. The assertion is true.
b. The assertion stems from a mistaken belief.

c. There's confusion with England and America's partnership.
d. Mr. Pelham has been wrongly convicted.

PART B

What POV is the statement written in?

a. Second-person
b. First-person

c. Third-person
d. Fourth-person

14. What does the term *connexion* mean?

a. Argument
b. Contact

c. Connection
d. Color

Use the following table from *The Voyager of the Beagle* by Charles Dickens (1839) to answer questions 15 to 20.

Name of Island.	Total No. of Species	No. of Species found in other parts of the world.	No. of Species confined to the Galapagos Archipelago.	No. confined to the one Island.	No. of Species confined to the Galapagos Archipelago, but found on more than the one Island.
James Island	71	33	38	30	8
Albemarle Island	46	18	26	22	4
Chatham Island	32	16	16	12	4
Charles Island	68	39 (or 29, if the probably imported plants be subtracted)	29	21	8

15. Which two islands have an equal number of species found on more than one island but confined to the Galapagos Archipelago?
    a. Chatham and Albermarle
    b. Abermarle and Charles
    c. Charles and Chatham
    d. Chatham and James

16. How many species are confined to Charles Island?

    a. 68
    b. 29
    c. 39
    d. 21

17. If the total number of species between the islands amounts to 217, what percentage of the total number does Albemarle have?

    a. About 5%
    b. About 20%
    c. About 50%
    d. About 75%

18. Which island has the highest number of species confined to the Galapagos Archipelago?

    a. Chatham Island
    b. Albemarle Island
    c. James Island
    d. Charles Island

19. How many imported plant species does Charles Island have?

    a. 10
    b. 29

    c. 39
    d. 15

20. Fill in the blanks with the most suitable **transition word or phrase** from the list below:

(in fact, consequently, for example)

a. There are other factors that could lead to violence besides video games. _____, poor mental health could cause violent behavior.

b. There is no homework tonight; _____, there has been no homework all week.

c. Mother didn't have time to go to the store; _____, there was no milk in the refrigerator.

> **Read the following excerpt from *The Wonderful Wizard of Oz* by L. Frank Baum (1901) and answer questions 21 to 26.**
>
> Forthwith, there was heard a great buzzing in the air, and a swarm of black bees came flying toward her.
>
> "Go to the strangers and sting them to death!" commanded the Witch, and the bees turned and flew rapidly until they came to where Dorothy and her friends were walking. But the Woodman had seen them coming, and the Scarecrow had decided what to do.
>
> "Take out my straw and scatter it over the little girl and the dog and the Lion," he said to the Woodman, "and the bees cannot sting them." This the Woodman did, and as Dorothy lay close beside the Lion and held Toto in her arms, the straw covered them entirely.
>
> The bees came and found no one but the Woodman to sting, so they flew at him and broke off all their stings against the tin, without hurting the Woodman at all. And as bees cannot live when their stings are broken, that was the end of the black bees, and they lay scattered thick about the Woodman, like little heaps of fine coal.

Then Dorothy and the Lion got up, and the girl helped the Tin Woodman put the straw back into the Scarecrow again, until he was as good as ever. So they started upon their journey once more.

The Wicked Witch was so angry when she saw her black bees in little heaps like fine coal that she stamped her foot and tore her hair and gnashed her teeth. And then she called a dozen of her slaves, who were the Winkies, and gave them sharp spears, telling them to go to the strangers and destroy them.

The Winkies were not a brave people, but they had to do as they were told. So they marched away until they came near to Dorothy. Then the Lion gave a great roar and sprang towards them, and the poor Winkies were so frightened that they ran back as fast as they could.

When they returned to the castle the Wicked Witch beat them well with a strap, and sent them back to their work, after which she sat down to think what she should do next. She could not understand how all her plans to destroy these strangers had failed; but she was a powerful Witch, as well as a wicked one, and she soon made up her mind how to act.

There was, in her cupboard, a Golden Cap, with a circle of diamonds and rubies running round it. This Golden Cap had a charm. Whoever owned it could call three times upon the Winged Monkeys, who would obey any order they were given. But no person could command these strange creatures more than three times. Twice already the Wicked Witch had used the charm of the Cap. Once was when she had made the Winkies her slaves, and set herself to rule over their country. The Winged Monkeys had helped her do this. The second time was when she had fought against the Great Oz himself, and driven him out of the land of the West. The Winged Monkeys had also helped her in doing this. Only once more could she use this Golden Cap, for which reason she did not like to do so until all her other powers were exhausted. But now that her fierce wolves and her wild crows and her stinging bees were gone, and her slaves had been scared away by the Cowardly Lion, she saw there was only one way left to destroy Dorothy and her friends.

So the Wicked Witch took the Golden Cap from her cupboard and placed it upon her head. Then she stood upon her left foot and said slowly:

"Ep-pe, pep-pe, kak-ke!"

Next she stood upon her right foot and said:

"Hil-lo, hol-lo, hel-lo!"

After this she stood upon both feet and cried in a loud voice:

"Ziz-zy, zuz-zy, zik!"

Now the charm began to work. The sky was darkened, and a low rumbling sound was heard in the air. There was a rushing of many wings, a great chattering and laughing, and the sun came out of the dark sky to show the Wicked Witch surrounded by a crowd of monkeys, each with a pair of immense and powerful wings on his shoulders.

21. **PART A**
    What is the main idea in this extract?

a. The Wicked Witch was determined to destroy Dorothy and her counterparts.

b. The Wicked Witch was determined to kill her black bees.

c. The Winkies had enslaved the Witch.

d. The Wicked Witch was successful in destroying Dorothy and her counterparts.

PART B

Which of the following sentences from the passage supports your answer to PART A?

a. And as bees cannot live when their stings are broken, that was the end of the black bees, and they lay scattered thick about the Woodman, like little heaps of fine coal.

b. She could not understand how all her plans to destroy these strangers had failed;

c. But no person could command these strange creatures more than three times.

d. The Winkies were not a brave people, but they had to do as they were told. So they marched away until they came near to Dorothy.

22. Who are the Winkies?

   a. A group of people destined to die for the Wicked Witch

   b. The Wicked Witch's sons

   c. The Wicked Witch's soldiers

   d. The Wicked Witch's slaves

23. Which of the following characters is NOT traveling with Dorothy?

   a. Woodman

   b. Toto

   c. Metalman

   d. Lion

24. What does the writer mean in this statement?

The bees came and found no one but the Woodman to sting, so they flew at him and broke off all their stings against the tin, without hurting the Woodman at all.

   a. The bees were too small to hurt the Woodman.

   b. The bees avoided stinging the Woodman.

   c. The Woodman swatted the bees until they all died.

   d. The Woodman's body is made of tin; therefore, the bees broke their stingers trying to sting him.

25. With what did the Wicked Witch beat the Winkies?

   a. A belt

   b. A shoe

   c. A strap

   d. Her hand

26. **PART A**

What foot was the Wicked Witch standing on when she said, "Hil-lo, hol-lo, hel-lo!"?

   a. Left foot

   b. Right foot

   c. Both feet

   d. None as she was sitting

PART B

What is the purpose of uttering these words?

   a. To call upon the Winkies

   b. To call upon the Winged Monkeys

   c. To curse Dorothy

   d. To calm herself

The following is a flyer distributed by trade unions for a boycott in 1898. Read it and answer questions 27 to 30.

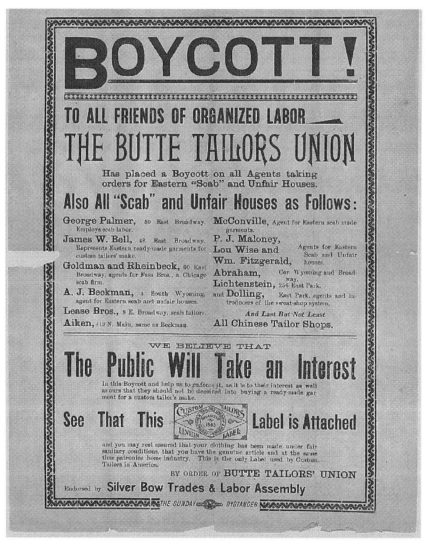

(Source: The Digital Public Library of America)

27. **PART A**

What is the purpose of this flyer?
a. To advertise the arrival of new materials to build houses
b. To announce Butte Tailors as the new governor
c. To announce a boycott on agents taking orders from Eastern "scab" and Unfair Houses
d. To announce an agreement between agents and Eastern "scab" and Unfair Houses

PART B

What must people ensure they do to enforce this decision?
a. Ensure their clothing has been tailored by their parents
b. Ensure their clothing has been hand-pressed
c. Ensure their clothing has the label as shown in the flyer
d. Ensure their clothing is washed every day

28. Who has endorsed this flyer?

a. Butte Tailor's Union
b. Silver Bow Trades and Labor Assembly
c. Silver Bow Trades Union
d. The Sunday Bystander

29. Which of the following IS NOT listed as an Eastern "Scab" and Unfair House?

    a. Wm. Fitzgerald
    b. Lichtendolly
    c. Lease Bros.
    d. Aiken.

30. Where was Goldman and Rheinbeck located?

    a. 60 East Broadway
    b. 256 East Park
    c. 50 East Broadway
    d. 50 East Broadway

31. Read the following sentence.

> *Once Cory picked up his pen and began writing, the essay became easy.*

If we change the start of the sentence to:

Writing the essay became easy ………..

What will the ending be?
    a. after starting.
    b. after picking up his pen.
    c. after Cory picked up his pen and began.
    d. after he finished the essay.

32. What does this proverb suggest?

> *A bird in the hand is worth two in the bush.*

    a. Your own possessions are always worth more to you.
    b. Birds are hard to catch, so hang on to one if you catch it.
    c. To have something is better than having nothing at all.
    d. A trained bird is twice the value of an untrained one.

33. **PART A**

What does the underlined word mean?

> *Tanya was a __morose__ woman, so people tended to avoid her.*

    a. Sullen
    b. Cheerful
    c. Childish
    d. Slow

PART B

What would you suggest for Tanya to do to make sure people want to be around her?

    a. To walk faster

    b. To be sad

    c. To get angrier

    d. To be friendly

Read the following passage from *Men of Invention and Industry* by Samuel Smiles (1885), and answer questions 34 to 40.

The use of iron in shipbuilding had small beginnings, like everything else. The established prejudice—that iron must necessarily sink in water—long continued to prevail against its employment. The first iron vessel was built and launched about a hundred years since by John Wilkinson, of Bradley Forge, in Staffordshire. In a letter of his, dated the 14th July, 1787, the original of which we have seen, he writes: "Yesterday week my iron boat was launched. It answers all my expectations, and has convinced the unbelievers, who were 999 in 1000. It will be only a nine days' wonder, and afterwards a Columbus's egg." It was, however, more than a nine days' wonder; for wood long continued to be thought the only material capable of floating.

Although Wilkinson's iron vessels continued to ply upon the Severn, more than twenty years elapsed before another shipbuilder ventured to follow his example. But in 1810, Onions and Son, of Brosely, built several iron vessels, also for use upon the Severn. Then, in 1815, Mr. Jervons, of Liverpool, built a small iron boat for use on the Mersey. Six years later, in 1821, Mr. Aaron Manby designed an iron steam vessel, which was built at the Horsley Company's Works, in Staffordshire. She sailed from London to Havre a few years later, under the command of Captain (afterwards Sir Charles) Napier, RN. She was freighted with a cargo of linseed and iron castings, and went up the Seine to Paris. It was some time, however, before iron came into general use. Ten years later, in 1832, Maudslay and Field built four iron vessels for the East India Company. In the course of about twenty years, the use of iron became general, not only for ships of war, but for merchant ships plying to all parts of the world.

When ships began to be built of iron, it was found that they could be increased without limit, so long as coal, iron, machinery, and strong men full of skill and industry, were procurable. The trade in shipbuilding returned to Britain, where iron ships are now made and exported in large numbers; the mercantile marine of this country exceeding in amount and tonnage that of all the other countries of the world put together. The "wooden walls" of England exist no more, for iron has superseded wood. Instead of constructing vessels from the forest, we are now digging new navies out of the bowels of the earth, and our "walls," instead of wood, are now of iron and steel.

The attempt to propel ships by other means than sails and oars went on from century to century, and did not succeed until almost within our own time. It is said that the Roman army under Claudius Codex was transported into Sicily in boats propelled by wheels moved by oxen. Galleys, propelled by wheels in paddles, were afterwards attempted. The Harleian MS. contains an Italian book of sketches, attributed to the 15th century, in which there appears a drawing of a paddle-boat, evidently intended to be worked by men. Paddle-boats, worked by horse-power, were also tried. Blasco Garay made a supreme effort at Barcelona in 1543. His vessel was propelled by a paddle-wheel on each side, worked by forty men. But nothing came of the experiment.

34. **PART A**

What is the main idea of this passage?

a. Iron is an excellent material for shipbuilding.

b. Iron is the best material to make shoes.

c. The use of Iron makes ships sink.

d. Wood is best for shipbuilding.

PART B

Which of the following sentences from the passage supports your answer to PART A?

a. The attempt to propel ships by other means than sails and oars went on from century to century, and did not succeed until almost within our own time.

b. In the course of about twenty years, the use of iron became general, not only for ships of war, but for merchant ships plying to all parts of the world.

c. The use of iron in shipbuilding had small beginnings, like everything else.

d. The Harleian MS. contains an Italian book of sketches, attributed to the 15th century, in which there appears a drawing of a paddle-boat, evidently intended to be worked by men.

35. What material was thought to be the only one to be able to float?

    a. Steel
    b. Iron
    c. Wood
    d. Silk

36. How was the Roman Army transported to Sicily?

    a. On planes
    b. In boats propelled by men
    c. In boats propelled by women
    d. In boats propelled by oxen

37. Who invented the double-hulled boat?

    a. Patrick Miller
    b. Claudius Codex

    c. Onions and Son
    d. East India company

38. **PART A**

Where did Aaron Manby build an iron steam vessel?

    a. Horsley and Horsley
    b. Horsley Company's Works
    c. Mersey
    d. Severn

PART B

In what direction did this ship first travel?

    a. Paris- London
    b. London- Havre
    c. Paris- Seine
    d. Seine- Paris

39. **PART A**

What does the writer mean by the following sentence?

*When ships began to be built of iron, it was found that they could be increased without limit, so long as coal, iron, machinery, and strong men full of skill and industry, were **procurable**.*

    a. Ships needed additional elements to function at maximum capacity.
    b. Ships needed to be weighed down to function at maximum capacity.
    c. Ships needed only strong men to function at maximum capacity.
    d. Ships were unreliable means of transport.

PART B

Which of the following options is an antonym for the underlined word?

    a. Available
    b. Unavailable

    c. Expensive
    d. Dire

40. What does the writer mean in the following sentence?

The "wooden walls" of England exist no more, for iron has superseded wood.

a. Iron is more expensive than wood.
b. England wasted its effort on using Iron to build ships.

c. Iron is used more frequently than wood to build ships.
d. The walls around England are made of wood.

---------   **THE END-**   ---------

ANSWER KEYS FOR THE PRACTICE EXERCISES

LESSON 2

Exercise 1
1. *Ferocity* means brutality.
2. *Atrocious* means shocking and cruel.
3. *Desolate* means to be empty or uninhabited.

Looking for the Root Word
2. The other word is "writing," in which the root word is "write." This means to mark words on a surface, such as paper.

Practice Exercise
1. The passage is about a black man and people's misconceptions and unkind reactions toward him.
2. "Unasked" means to have not queried about something.
3. I broke down the word to its parts to figure out the meaning.
4.

Un-	-ask-	-ed
Prefix	Root word	Suffix

5.

WHICH WORDS HAVE PREFIXES?	WHICH WORDS HAVE SUFFIXES?
Unasked **Half**-hesitant **Out**rages	Unask**ed** Feel**ings** Delica**cy** Difficul**ty** Right**ly** Fram**ing** Direct**ly** Compassionate**ly** Outrag**es**

6. One can infer that Mr. Brainley does not enjoy walking around his neighborhood.
7. The suffix in the word "occasionally" is "-ly" while the suffix in "teenage" is "-age."
8. a. "-Hood" refers to an area where a group of people live close by.
   b. "-Ish" means to be of a certain nationality.
9. a. "Animosity" means a feeling of dislike or hatred.
   b. "Minions" refer to the servants of a powerful person.
   c. "Venerable" means to be wise due to age.
   d. "Hackneyed" means to be overused.

10.

WORD	PREFIX	ROOT WORD	SUFFIX	MEANING
Megaphone	Mega-	Phone		A device that makes one's voice louder when one speaks into it
Incapable	In-	Capable		To be unable to do something
Psychology		Psyche	-ology	The study of the human mind
Hypercritical	Hyper-	Critic	-al	To be an excessively harsh judge
Productive		Product	-ive	To be getting a lot done
Excellence		Excel	-ence	The quality of being outstanding
Contradictory		Contradict	-ory	To be inconsistent or opposite

LESSON 3

Exercise 1
1. Javan Rhinos are extinct because they have been killed.
2. The business needed to close for a month because the employees were on strike.

Exercise 2
1. Therefore
2. Yes, it is an appropriate rewrite. In the two sentences, the boys playing in the rain is the cause. The effect is that they became sick.

Exercise 3
1. I took a step back and evaluated the situation, as opposed to making an assumption and making things worse.
2. Katherine has worn green Adidas shoes just like Felix.

Exercise 4
1. In the summer and fall of 1777, British General, John Burgoyne, led eight thousand soldiers through the Hudson Valley towards Saratoga, New York.
2. In February 1778, the French entered the war.

3.

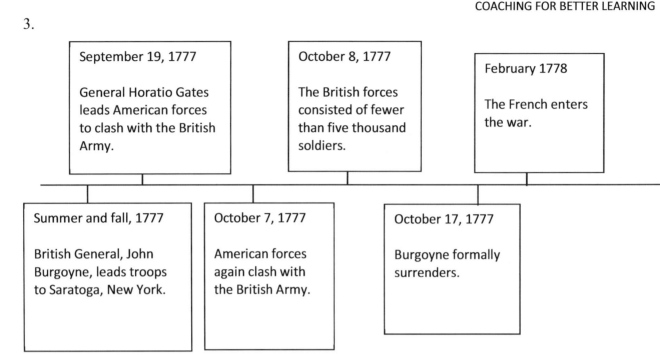

September 19, 1777

General Horatio Gates leads American forces to clash with the British Army.

October 8, 1777

The British forces consisted of fewer than five thousand soldiers.

February 1778

The French enters the war.

Summer and fall, 1777

British General, John Burgoyne, leads troops to Saratoga, New York.

October 7, 1777

American forces again clash with the British Army.

October 17, 1777

Burgoyne formally surrenders.

4. I can infer that the Americans were in a battle with the British and were winning. Upon Burgoyne's surrender, the French enters to support the Americans and help them win the war.

Exercise 5
One can infer that the writer believed there was a general consensus that America should one day be independent and separated from England. However, people's opinions on when the separation should occur varied.

Practice Exercise
1. a. "Consequently" and "as a result" are linking words.
   b. **Cause:** Kate's performance was affected by her increasing health issues.
   Effects: Consequently, her supervisor sat down with her to discuss ways in which the company could accommodate her. As a result, she has a flexible work schedule and sometimes works from home.

2. a. I can infer that a man has a problem that he wishes Mr. Holmes to solve as he considers Mr. Holmes the second-best expert in Europe. Mr. Holmes is insulted by the ranking, but the man assures him that he is the only one who can solve matters as a practical man.

   b. The writer uses the compare and contrast structure by comparing Mr. Holmes to Monsieur Bertillon. In precise information and science, Mr. Holmes rank second to Bertillon. However, in practical issues, Bertillon cannot be compared to Mr. Holmes.

3. The cause is addressed before the effect. The person wishes to examine the other, which causes him to call the other the previous night and that day.

4. a. This is a compare and contrast text structure.

b. The passage compares chemical and physical changes on matter. While physical changes do not alter the make-up of matter, chemicals can transform matter to a different form with different features.

5. a. The author arrived on February 16th.

b. The circumference is under three-quarters of a mile.

c. Chemical and mechanical changes from volcanoes have caused the islands to be composed of either coral or erupted matter.

d. The majority of islands are situated near seacoasts or as islands in the midst of the sea.

6. a. It has a cause and effect structure.

b. The writer begins with the effect, which is the economy being in disarray in 2008. They then list three causes of this occurrence, which are easy credit conditions, the sale of toxic loans by banks and the backing and misrepresentation of these loans by insurance firms.

LESSON 4

Exercise 1
This text reminds me of my aunt who would visit our childhood home sometimes. She was critical of how we cooked our food, and the house was never clean enough in her opinion.

Exercise 2
In both excerpts, the men being described are tall, thin and seem to have affectionate personalities.

Exercise 3
The excerpt reminds me of the times when people are advised to remain indoors due to impending storms and hurricanes.

Practice Exercises
1. a. I act like the character when I am exhausted as I can become forgetful and feel frustrated and stuck when facing any obstacle.

b. This reminds me of the time my computer malfunctioned, and I lost a project that I stayed up many nights working on. I felt overwhelmed and hopeless.

c. This excerpt reminds me of *The Secret Garden*, in which the character, Mary Lennox, finds the key to a mysterious garden.

2. a. Love and marriage come to mind when I read these two excerpts.
    b. The excerpts remind me of another one Jane Austen's novel, *Mansfield Park*, due to the themes of love and marriage.

c. The excerpts remind me that the marriage rate in the U.S. is declining over the years. They also remind me of the rise in self-help books that offer advice on attracting partners and having successful romantic relationships.

3. a. The picture reminds me of the times I must catch a bus or train during rush hours.

b. The picture reminds me that there are still numerous conflicts ongoing in the world today, such as the conflict in Ukraine, the war in Afghanistan and the war in Yemen.

LESSON 5

Exercise 1
1. The stuffed toy represents the child's innocence.
2. The red flowers represent Chris' love.

Exercise 2
-   "We shall walk with a walk that is measured and slow / and watch where the chalk-white arrows go"- Shel Silverstein in the poem, "Where the Sidewalk Ends"
-   "Many mumbling mice are making midnight music in the moonlight"- Dr. Seuss in Dr. Seuss's ABC
-   "I've been a puppet, a pauper, a pirate, a poet, a pawn and a king"- Frank Sinatra in "That's Life"

Exercise 3
1. The snow is so deep that I think it might be deeper than the Mariana Trench!
2. It is so hot that I feel like I am melting.

Exercise 4
1. a. When his sister tried to pick up his phone, Marco grabbed it as quick as a cat.
    b. Although she was small and soft-spoken, Elise was as tough as nails.

2. a. like a fish in the ocean
    b. like an angel

Exercise 5
1. Reality is his worst enemy sometimes.
    Reality is compared to his worst enemy.

2. The principal's announcement of the holiday was music to the students' ears.
    The principal's announcement is compared to music.

Practice Exercises
1. a. "My feet were killing me" really means that my feet were very painful.

    b. "Worked my fingers to the bone" really means that I worked very hard.

    c. "Dying to see" really means that I was longing see the movie.

    d. "I was so tired that I couldn't move" really means that I was very exhausted.

2.   a. When I read the poem, the power of love comes to mind.

    b. Examples of hyperbole are "live coiled in shells of loneliness," "ancient histories of pain" and "yet it is only love/ which sets us free."

    c. The examples of alliteration include "love leaves," "high holy," "old memories of pleasure/ ancient histories of pain," "we are weaned," "suddenly we see" and "we are/ and will ever be."

3.   a. Metaphor
     b. Simile
     c. Metaphor
     d. Simile

4.   Lacy and her brother went to the market on Monday evening. While they were walking, <u>it began to rain so much, they felt like they were under a waterfall.</u> By the time they entered the door, <u>they were soaked as though they had been thrown into the sea.</u> Lacy selected a shopping trolley, but its wheels were squeaky. <u>They wobbled all around as though trying to flee from beneath the trolley.</u> Her brother quickly selected the groceries on the list. Although they didn't have many items, <u>they had to recheck to be sure they weren't paying for a Ferrari.</u> They grabbed the bags of groceries, <u>which felt like bags of concrete bricks,</u> and returned   home.

5.   a. The spider weaving its web is the symbol.
     b. This may be a reference to the saying "oh what a tangled web we weave when first we practice to deceive" by Sir Walter Scott. Therefore, the spider weaving its web may represent the lies Daniel is telling Carol.

LESSON 6

Practice Exercise
Passage 1
  1. Part A: Guernica refers to a small town in northern Spain and it also refers to Picasso's painting.

Part B: In the introductory paragraph, Guernica is referred to as a painting that "was the response of the Spanish-born artist, Pablo Picasso, to the bombing of Guernica, a small Basque town in northern Spain."

2. **b. Picasso's painting was a response based on the bombing of Guernica.**
   Evidence: "The painting was the response of the Spanish-born artist, Pablo Picasso, to the bombing of Guernica, a small Basque town in northern Spain that was destroyed on April 26, 1937…"
   c. An example of Cubism painting technique is using a compressed pictorial space.
   Evidence: "Picasso's compressed pictorial space and fragmented forms are characteristic of Cubism."

3. a.

4. Part A: c
   Part B: d

5. Part A: The main idea of the passage is that Pablo Picasso created a painting, Guernica, to make viewers reflect on the effects of the war after the attack on the Spanish town.

   Part B:
   - "First shown at the 1937 International Exposition in Paris, Guernica stands today as a universal statement against the horror of modern warfare."
   - "The painting was the response of the Spanish-born artist, Pablo Picasso, to the bombing of Guernica, a small Basque town in northern Spain…"
   - "The monochromatic color scheme recalls Cubism, but also the black and white newspapers that broadcast the devastating effects of the bombing around the world."

6. The painting styles Picasso used are cubism and surrealism.

7.

WHAT HAVE I LEARNED?
- Guernica was destroyed on April 26, 1937 during the Spanish Civil War.
- There was international public outcry following the bombing.
- The attack was one of the first demonstrations of a full-scale aerial bombing.
- Images of the bombing changed people's perceptions of war and its harsh effects on humanity.
- Picasso's painting led people to reflect more deeply on war.

Passage 2

1. a. *Certain-ty*
   b. *Precise-ly*
   c. *Local-ity*
   d. *Singular-ly*

2. The most remarkable feature is that the different islands differ, to a large extent, in the animals that inhabit them.

3. Mr. Lawson first saw this in tortoises.

4. The main idea in this passage is that the islands in the South American archipelago have different species of the same animals.

5. Darwin did not pay much attention at first to Mr. Lawson's observation.

6. Darwin thought that he and Mr. Gray were unable to find any specific differences because the specimens were young.

7. Darwin's attention was "first thoroughly aroused" when he compared the numerous specimens of the mocking-thrushes.

8. The specimens of the finch tribe were mingled together.

9.

WHAT HAVE I LEARNT
- Although the islands of the South American archipelago seemed identical in their features, different species of the same animals inhabited them.
- The inhabitants of the islands were able to identify the different species.
- In some cases, none of the islands had the same species.

LESSON 7

1. Part A: b
   Part B: Thomas took a long time to complete his homework.

2. Part A: d
   Part B: Fortunate lady

3. a. overspread: cover
   b. returned: replied
   c. carpet-bag: traveling bag
   d. mackintosh: a raincoat
   e. stout: strong and thick
   f. native: of a person's birth
   g. chary: cautious
   h. hitherto: until then

i. wardrobes: clothes

4. Part A: Mr. Fogg is an eccentric man.
   Part B: Mr. Fogg is eccentric as he believes that he can travel around the world in eighty days and states that he will only carry two shirts and three stockings.

5. Yes, Passepartout misses being home as the passage states, "After all, Passepartout, who had been away from France five years, would not be sorry to set foot on his native soil again."

6. Part A: d

   Part B: The passage states that "until Wendy came, her mother was the chief one." It is also stated that her mother's mind was like boxes filled with boxes, suggesting that she was complex.

7. c

8. The word "conspicuous" means to be very noticeable. This is evident as the passage states exactly where Wendy sees the kiss in the "right-hand corner."

9. Part A: The main idea is that Mrs. Darling was an assertive, complex woman who withheld love from her child and husband.

   Part B: i. It is stated that Mrs. Darling is the "chief one."
   ii. Mrs. Darling's mind is likened to tiny boxes with one within the other. According to the passage, "however many you discover there is always one more."
   iii. The passage also states that Mrs. Darling held a kiss that her husband had given up trying to get and Wendy could never get.

10. a. Jade feels like she could be sick, **so** she asks her mother to take her to the hospital. On their way to the hospital, the car tire bursts **due to** a stray nail on the road. They have no option **but to** call an ambulance.

    b. Alan refers to himself as a comedian, **but** he is not funny. He makes crude jokes **that** most people do not like. **Both** his brother and wife have asked him to choose another career.

11.

WORD	PREFIX	ROOT WORD	SUFFIX	MEANING
Fertility		Fertile	ity	Having the ability to produce young
Physician		Physic	ian	A person who practices medicine
Superficial		Super	ficial	To be near the surface; shallow
Nonsense	Non	Sense		To not be sensible
Intermission	Inter	Mission		A break between the parts of a movie or play

12. Simile

LESSON 8
Practice Exercises

1. Edison's work has benefited humanity in many ways as it has contributed to the invention of certain tools and connected science to daily life.

2. Part A: The stranger was unpleasant to the narrator and expected him to obey his every command.

    Part B: The narrator notes that the stranger's expression "was not at all pleasant." He also states that if he did not obey the man quickly enough, he was reprimanded.

3. An appropriate title is "At the Mercy of a Stranger."

4. Part A: The main idea is that flower petals close during the summer night.

    Part B: The speaker says, "Now sleeps the crimson petal, now the white" and "Now folds the lily all her sweetness up" to indicate that the flower petals are closing. He also says that "the firefly wakens" to describe the activities of the firefly.

5. Another appropriate title is "The Flowers Take Their Rest."

6. The image shows the COVID-19 statistics of Latvia on 31st May, 2020.

7. The image shows the number of Latvian people tested for the COVID-19 virus, the number and percentage of the population that were tested positive, and the number of people that succumbed to the virus.

8. An appropriate title will be "Latvia COVID-19 Update for 31st May, 2020."

9.

WHAT DID I KNOW ABOUT THIS TOPIC?	WHAT DID I WANT TO KNOW?	WHAT HAVE I LEARNT?
I knew that World War II ended in 1945. I knew that the Trinity test was the first nuclear weapon test.	I wanted to know the effects of the test on people and the environment.	I learnt that the explosion was so intense that it obscured people's vision with light and clouds.

10. I can infer that the bomb test was so huge and intense that it was seen and felt miles from the site.

11. The main idea is that the Trinity bomb test of 1945 was severe and obscured the vision of people who were miles away

12. Another appropriate title will be "My Experience with the 1945 Trinity Bomb Test."

LESSON 9

Exercise 1
1. Indirect: Whenever he passes her desk, Denise deeply inhales his heavenly, sweet cologne.
2. Indirect: It was no surprise that Sonya aced the test when the rest of us barely passed.
3. Direct: The man was homeless.
4. Direct: She was heartless.

Exercise 2
1. Part A: The scenario occurred in a supermarket.
   Part B: The character is pushing a cart down aisles, which are found in supermarkets. The mother is placing packages and boxes in the cart, which suggests that she is selecting packaged foods and placing them into the cart.

2. i. The cart will become too heavy for the character to continue pushing.
   ii. The character will crash the cart into a shelf because he will be having too much difficulty controlling the cart.

3. I can infer that the ships and airplanes are perhaps going on a war mission. As propeller airplanes were frequently used around the 1940s, I can also infer that the events are taking place around the time of World War II.

Exercise 3
1. i. John is unloving as it is stated that he "had not much affection for his mother and sisters."
   ii. John is also cruel as he bullies the narrator every chance he gets. She states that he bullied her "continually" and she feared him.
2. i. Jane is ten years old whereas John is fourteen years old.
   ii. She is timid and fearful of him while he is cruel.

Practice Exercises
1. Huck's clothes were men's discarded clothing.

2. Huck held up his pants with one suspender.

3. Huck never had to take a bath.

4. No one told Huck what to do.

5. Huck went barefoot in the spring.

6. Part A: i. Weena is childish.
　　ii. She is weak.
　　　　iii. She is fearful.
　　　　iv. She is affectionate.
　　　　v. She is devoted to the narrator.

　　Part B: i. The narrator states that she is "exactly like a child."
　　　　ii. She gets tired easily.
　　　　iii. She becomes distressed whenever the narrator leaves her.
　　　　iv. She shows the narrator affection in her "weak, futile way."
　　　　v. She tries to follow the narrator everywhere he goes.

7. Part A: i. He is sympathetic.
　　ii. He is impatient.

　　Part B: i. He feels guilty for tiring her out.
　　ii. He states that he "had as much trouble as comfort from her devotion."

LESSON 10

Exercise 1

1. I imagine a wrecking ball breaking down walls.

2. The song is about a person who is trying to reach out to another who is resisting her attempts and has closed off their feelings. As a result, the person feels hurt and vulnerable.

Exercise 2

1. I can see a bird soaring in the sky in the sun's orange rays. I can also see another bird with clipped wings that is singing from a locked cage.

2. The poem highlights the different experiences of the oppressed and those who have freedom and power.

Practice Exercise

1. a. The events are taking place during autumn or fall.

　　b. The F-16 is a fighter aircraft that is being used during battle.

2. a. The song is about two people trying to make a relationship work but failing to do so.

　　b. The image formed is of two people slowly dancing in a room that is on fire.

　　c. "Failed relationships" is the theme.

d. Yes, the lyrics remind me of a past relationship in which my partner and I tried our best to compromise and work things out before deciding to part ways.

3. a. The loneliness and harshness of a city during winter comes to mind.

    b. The images that come to mind are "withered leaves," discarded newspapers in "vacant lots," "broken blinds," "a cab-horse" and "lamps."

    c. Yes, auditory imagery can be found in the line "A lonely cab-horse steams and stamps."

    d. Loneliness is the theme of the poem.

4. a. I learned that the writer grew up in the suburbs of a city in Ontario in a box-shaped house with a well-manicured lawn.

    b. The text reminds me of my home in the suburbs. We had a garden and I often caught ladybugs in it.

    c. While reading the excerpt, I imagine the well-maintained house and lawn where the narrator lived. I also imagine the field of tall grasses, milkweed leaves and the black, yellow and white butterflies.

    d. She is intrigued by the monarch caterpillar's colors and docile behavior. Therefore, she picks it up and carries it home.

LESSON 11

Exercise 1
The use of the first-person pronouns "I," "we," "our" and "my" indicates that it was written in the first-person narrative.

Exercise 2
The passage only uses third-person pronouns such as "they," "he" and "his."

Exercise 3
1. He recorded that he was born (as he has been informed and believe) on a Friday, at twelve o'clock at night. It was remarked that the clock began to strike, and he began to cry, simultaneously.

2. Since my papa's death, I had found out that it was best not to talk to my mamma about him. When my father was ill, I had been sent away, and when he had returned, everything was over...

Practice Exercise
1. a. first-person

      b. first-person

      c. first-person

      d. third-person

2. But I was neither house-dog nor kennel-dog. The whole realm was mine. I plunged into the swimming tank or went hunting with the Judge's sons; I escorted Mollie and Alice, the Judge's daughters, on long twilight or early morning rambles; on wintry nights I lay at the Judge's feet before the roaring library fire; I carried the Judge's grandsons on my back, or rolled them in the grass, and guarded their footsteps through wild adventures down to the fountain in the stable yard, and even beyond, where the paddocks were, and the berry patches. Among the terriers I stalked imperiously, and Toots and Ysabel I utterly ignored, for I was king, —king over all creeping, crawling, flying things of Judge Miller's place, humans included.

3. It was two o'clock when I came to myself and called for the police. The murderer was gone long ago; but there lay his victim in the middle of the lane, incredibly mangled. Horrified, I observed that the stick with which the deed had been done, although it was of some rare and very tough and heavy wood, had broken in the middle under the stress of this insensate cruelty; and one splintered half had rolled in the neighboring gutter. The other had been carried away by the murderer. I found a purse and gold watch upon the victim: but no cards or papers, except a sealed and stamped envelope, which he had been probably carrying to the post, and which bore the name and address of Mr. Utterson.

LESSON 12

1. a. The author is a professor of psychology at Harvard University.
   b. The book was published in 1918.
   c. The book is Volume 1.

2. Students are the intended audience.

3. a. The book includes six chapters.
   b. Chapter III, "The Old West," is the longest chapter.

4. "Thompson, D.G." is covered extensively.

5. The heading is "The Relations of Minds to Other Things."

6. a. "The Psychologist's Point of View" starts on page 218.
   b. "Introspection" falls under the heading "The Methods ands Snares of Psychology."

7. The keywords include *re-education, a priori probability, thalami and corpora quadrigemina.*

8. The image from *The Principles of Psychology* is an illustration of a brain. The image from *Personal Memoirs of U.S. Grant* is a captured image of a letter.

9. The illustration shows afferent and efferent paths in the brain.

10. There are four columns.

11. There are 39 people missing from Raymond.

12. It falls under the social, self-seeking section.

13. Champion's Hill has the highest number of wounded people.

14. I can infer that absolute self-consciousness, reason or experience includes the transcendental ego and the world, which are further divided.

15. Tennessee and Mississippi are two states.

16. Corinth is in Mississippi.

PRACTICE TEST ANSWER KEYS

	PART A	PART B		PART A	PART B		PART A	PART B		PART A	PART B
1	C	A	11	B	C	21	A		31	B	B
2	D		12	-Tele- (prefix) phone (root word) -Describe- (root word) -tion (suffix) -Art- (root word) -ist (suffix) -Dis (prefix) respect (root word)		22	B		32	A	D
3	C		13	A		23	B		33	C	
4	A	C	14	A		24	D	D	34	B	
5	D		15	C		25	B		35	A	A
6	B		16	A	D	26	B	C	36	C	
7	C	B	17	B	A	27	D		37	A	
8	B		18	C		28	B		38	C	B
9	A	C	19	A		29	D		39	A	
10	C		20	B		30	C		40	B	

	PART A	PART B		PART A	PART B		PART A	PART B		PART A	PART B
1	A	A	11	D		21	A	B	31	C	
2	D	C	12	C		22	D		32	C	
3	B		13	B	B	23	C		33	A	D
4	B	A	14	C		24	D		34	A	B
5	C		15	A		25	C		35	C	
6	D	C	16	D		26	B	B	36	D	
7	B	C	17	B		27	C	C	37	A	
8	a. none b. hyperbole c. hyperbole		18	C		28	B		38	B	B
9	D	B	19	A		29	B		39	A	B
10	B	C	20	a. for example b. in fact c. consequently		30	A		40	C	

REFERENCES AND EXCERPTS

Books

- *The Hound of the Baskervilles* by Sir Arthur Conan Doyle (1902)
- *The Souls of Black Folk* by W. E. B. Du Bois (1903)
- *Pride and Prejudice* by Jane Austen (1813)
- *The Strange Case of Dr. Jekyll and Mr. Hyde* by Robert Louis Stevenson (1866)
- *Alice's Adventures in Wonderland* by Lewis Carroll (1865)
- *Wuthering Heights* by Emily Bronte (1847)
- *Jane Eyre* by Charlotte Bronte (1847)
- *The Voyager of the Beagle* by Charles Dickens (1839)
- *Around the World in Eighty Days* by Jules Verne (1873)
- *Peter Pan* by James M. Barrie (1902)
- *Edison as I know Him* by Henry Ford (1930)
- *Treasure Island* by Robert Louis Stevenson (1883)
- *The Wonderful Wizard of Oz* by L. Frank Baum (1901)
- *The Adventures of Tom Sawyer* by Mark Twain (1876)
- *The Time Machine* by H.G Wells (1895)
- *Becoming His Mother* by Mary A. Scherf (2015)
- *True Crime* by Lee Gutkind (2013)
- *Finding Sanctuary in Butterfly Town, USA* by Jennifer Lunden (2011)
- *Black Beauty* by Anna Sewell (1877)
- *The Adventures of Tom Sawyer* by Mark Twain (1876)
- *Common Sense* by Thomas Paine (1776)
- *David Copperfield* by Charles Dickens (1850)
- *Little Lord Fauntleroy* by Frances Hodgson Burnett (1885)
- *The Call of the Wild* by Jack London (1903)
- *The Principles of Psychology* by William James (1890)
- *The Frontier in American History* by Frederick Turner (1920)
- *Personal Memoirs of U.S. Grant* by Ulysses S. Grant (1885)
- *Men of Invention and Industry* by Samuel Smiles (1885)

Articles

- Pablo Picasso's Guernica and Modern War: Sourced from Digital Public Library of America: https://dp.la/primary-source-sets/pablo-picasso-s-guernica-and-modern-war
- Cesar Chavez's vision of political and economic emancipation for farm workers, circa 1970 (poster): https://dp.la/primary-source-sets/the-united-farm-workers-and-the-delano-grape-strike/sources/1324
- The text of an eyewitness account of the Trinity bomb test, 1945 (poster and text): Sourced from https://dp.la/primary-source-sets/the-atomic-bomb-and-the-nuclear-age/sources/51
- An 1864 illustration depicting "The Modern Medea: The Story of Margaret Garner" (poster): Sourced from Digital Public Library of America: https://dp.la/primary-source-sets/beloved-by-toni-morrison/sources/579

- "Crimes Set to Music," an *All Star Comics* issue (Poster): Sourced from Digital Public Library of America: https://dp.la/primary-source-sets/truth-justice-and-the-birth-of-the-superhero-comic-book/sources/1523
- Fake News in the 1890s: Yellow Journalism: Sourced from Digital Public Library of America: https://dp.la/primary-source-sets/fake-news-in-the-1890s-yellow-journalism#tabs
- The Lady's Guide to Perfect Gentility, 1859: Sourced from Digital Public Library of America: https://dp.la/primary-source-sets/victorian-era/sources/1849
- Poem about women hand-knitting socks for Civil War soldiers: Sourced from Digital Public Library of America: https://dp.la/primary-source-sets/little-women-by-louisa-may-alcott/sources/167
- Advertisement published in The American Anti-Slavery Almanac, 1838: Sourced from Digital Public Library of America: https://dp.la/primary-source-sets/incidents-in-the-life-of-a-slave-girl-by-harriet-jacobs/sources/1131
- Flyer distributed by trade unions for a boycott of Chinese and Japanese--run businesses in 1898: Sourced from Digital Public Library of America: https://dp.la/primary-source-sets/early-chinese-immigration-to-the-us/sources/84
- "Mormon Migration" (article): Sourced from Digital Public Library of America: https://dp.la/primary-source-sets/mormon-migration
- "Revolutionary War Turning Points: Saratoga and Valley Forge" (article): Sourced from Digital Public Library of America: https://dp.la/primary-source-sets/revolutionary-war-turning-points-saratoga-and-valley-forge
- "There is No Cure for Polio" (article): Sourced from Digital Public Library of America: https://dp.la/primary-source-sets/there-is-no-cure-for-polio

Poems
- "Romeo and Juliet" by Shakespeare (1597)
- "Insomniac" by Maya Angelou (Date unknown)
- "To Kill a Mockingbird" by Harper Lee (1960)
- "Touched by an Angel" by Maya Angelou (1995)
- "The Raven" by Edgar Allan Poe (1845)
- "The Rose That Grew from Concrete" by Tupac Shakur (1999)
- "I Know Why the Caged Bird Sings" by Maya Angelou (1969)
- "Preludes" by T.S. Eliot (1911)
- "Alone With Everybody" by Charles Bukowski (1977)

Songs
- "Fireworks" by Katy Perry (2009)
- "When I Fall" by Barenaked Ladies (1996)
- "Wrecking Ball" by Miley Cyrus (2013)
- "Slow Dancing in a Burning Room" by John Mayer (2006)
- "Titanium" by David Guetta featuring Sia (2011)
- "Every Rose has Its Thorn" by Poison (1988)

ABOUT COACHING FOR BETTER LEARNING, LLC

CBL helps develop systems that increase performance and save time, resources, and energy.

If you identify typos and errors in the text, please let us know at **teamcbl@coachingforbetterlearning.com.** We promise to fix them and send you a free copy of the updated textbook to thank you.